Developing Learning
in Early Childhood

The 0–8 series

The 0–8 series edited by Professor Tina Bruce, deals with essential themes in early childhood which concern practitioners, parents and children. In a practical and accessible way, the series sets out a holistic approach to work with young children, families and their communities. It is evidence based, drawing on theory and research. The books are designed for use by early years practitioners, and those on professional development courses, and initial teacher education courses covering the age-range 0–8.

Series listing

Tina Bruce: *Developing Learning in Early Childhood* 2004
Mollie Davies: *Movement and Dance in Early Childhood*
2nd edition 2003
John Matthews: *Drawing and Painting: Children and Visual Representation*
2nd edition 2003
Marian Whitehead: *Developing Language and Literacy with Young Children*
2nd edition 2002
Rosemary Roberts: *Self-esteem and Early Learning* 2nd edition 2002
Cath Arnold: *Child Development and Learning 2–5 – Georgia's Story* 1999
Pat Gura: *Resources for Early Learning* 1997
Chris Pascal and Tony Bertram: *Effective Early Learning – Case Studies in Improvement* 1997

All titles are available from Paul Chapman Publishing
http://www/paulchapmanpublishing.co.uk

Sage Publications
www.sagepub.co.uk and www.sagepub.com

Developing Learning in Early Childhood

Tina Bruce

Los Angeles | London | New Delhi
Singapore | Washington DC

First published 2004

Reprinted 2009, 2010

SAGE Publications Ltd
1 Oliver's Yard
55 City Road
London EC1Y 1SP

SAGE Publications Inc.
2455 Teller Road
Thousand Oaks, California 91320

SAGE Publications India Pvt Ltd
B 1/I 1 Mohan Cooperative Industrial Area
Mathura Road
New Delhi 110 044

SAGE Publications Asia-Pacific Pte Ltd
33 Pekin Street #02-01
Far East Square
Singapore 048763

Library of Congress Control Number: 2003106582

A catalogue record for this book is available from the British Library

ISBN 978 0 7619 4175 0 (hbk)
ISBN 978 0 7619 4176 7 (pbk)

Typeset by Dorwyn Ltd, Rowlands Castle, Hants
Printed and bound by CPI Antony Rowe, Chippenham, Wiltshire

Contents

Dedication

This book is dedicated to Sheena Johnstone, who was a Senior Lecturer at Moray House College. She has been one of the great influences on the professional development of the people involved in developing learning in young children, their families and those who work with them.

Sheena did not see education as the teacher trying to change those he or she taught, whether they were children, parents or her students. Her approach to education was not a revolutionary one. Rather, she practised In the Froebelian tradition of sensitively observing, tuning in to the person, matching this with what they needed to learn, but often pitching it just above their level, thus causing them to think and learn.

It was by helping students and children to quietly reflect and transcend what they knew, understood and felt, that they became the agents of their own learning and often transformed themselves.

She would do this by giving an example. A little boy was pretending to be a David Attenborough character, and she was, at his request, the camera person. He described a robin, and then, face to camera (Sheena being the camera operator), said, 'I am returning you now to Sheena, in the studio.' She quickly assumed the part of the presenter. In sharing this experience, she helped practitioners and parents to consider the role of the adult in supporting and extending childhood play, and the richness of learning that it cultivates.

Those who studied and worked with Sheena are dotted about everywhere, for her influence remains. They can be identified for their quiet, solid, informed approach, their deep and sustained love and joy in children, and respect for and partnership with the families they work with.

These are not trendy practitioners, following every educational fashion with superficial enthusiasm. They will not be forced into ways of working with children which go against their considered, evidence-based philosophy. Neither are they are stuck in a rut, but seek, throughout their professional lives, that which develops their practice in the Froebelian spirit to which Sheena introduced them. Many of us grieve for her, but her influence will sustain the work that needs to be done.

Acknowledgements

It has been a huge task but a deep pleasure to round up the work and thinking we have done together in the Castlebrae Community Cluster in Edinburgh from 1999. What a team we have been together. We have all been leaders and followers according to the need of the moment, and hopefully we have moved the work of the community forward in the doing. What a long way we have travelled together since the conference we had in May 2001, where we came to the decision that we would make a book together.

We hope that the book will be useful to students and practitioners in diverse settings, as a core text, to support them in their work with children and families.

Our thanks to:

- City of Edinburgh Council Education Department for the ongoing support and interest
- City of Edinburgh Social Work Department for the ongoing interest and support
- New Community Schools budget for the funding that made it all possible
- Children, parents and staff in all the settings

Tina Bruce

Foreword

In *Children's Minds*, her famous little book on early learning, Margaret Donaldson wonders what happens after five to extinguish a child's natural enthusiasm for discovery and shared human sense, a talent so evident in a happy nursery school. Why does the primary-school experience often seem so hard? Why do so many children struggle to succeed, lose confidence or require 'special education' or discipline? What goes wrong with that cheerful 'disposition to learn' that Lilian Katz says is essential, which we believe is present in every boy and girl? Where has the 'collaborative learning' in 'communities of learners' of Jerome Bruner gone? Recently Barbara Rogoff and her colleagues have drawn attention to the historical events in the practical disciplining of industrial society that made the process of learning into instruction, that replaced the old tradition, by which children are expected to learn by intent participation in meaningful, useful occupations, with a factory model of education by assembly-line instruction. What is it about modern families and modern society that causes some parents to find children a puzzling burden, rather than a boon? Surely by nature they are affectionate companions who assure the healthy future of the community.

If children are born collaborators and creators, keen on learning meanings and tasks, proud of responsibility and generous participants in joint tasks, as infancy research leads us to believe, why do we have unhappy, rebellious, sad or angry inattenders in school, and exclusion, bullying and truancy? Why do more and more youngsters qualify as ADHD or autism spectrum disordered? Are they really just abnormal, or is their natural sociability being let down somehow? What is wrong with the management of early lives?

This book offers answers to such questions, and more. Tina Bruce tells the recent history of the natural and creative growth of a vital community of learners, of an experiment in collaborative education and social celebration of diverse experiences and skills that works to benefit young children, parents and practitioners in education and social services. I think the Castle-brae Community Cluster of Craigmillar is a model learning community, one that could instruct higher-level institutions of training for life in society, including, maybe, our universities.

It is a great story of work inspired by the principles of respect and encouragement for the natural vitality and collaborative intelligence of children that Sheena Johnstone promoted in a long and influential life as a teacher of teachers at Moray House College in Edinburgh. Teachers of young children discover that they do best if they are ready to imagine and discover and learn with their young companions, who are motivated to acquire any number of ways of thinking, doing and symbolizing if helped by someone who will listen, show, dance and dream with them. And parents are natural teachers and learners too, partners in the enjoyment of education.

At Craigmillar, four maintained nursery schools; three primary schools, a Books for Babies project, a family centre, two children's centres and a Healthy Eating project work together, discovering and inventing the process of learning and growth of socially valuable skills, and developing multi-agency collaboration. By means of in-service days and follow-up work on how children become symbol users from babyhood, practitioners and teachers develop first-hand experience of children representing, predicting and rearranging their experience. The Community Cluster held a conference in May 2001, 'Bairns Aboon A. Beyond Here and Now: The Development of Symbolic Behaviour', presenting videos, photographic summaries and artefacts to illustrate the children's experience. Parents took part as active partners.

Tina describes herself as a scribe for the work over three years, but this book is much more than just a record. It is a carefully thought out examination of a journey of discovery, and of the building of a philosophy of practice that includes every aspect of the many ways children in family and society may gain mastery of themselves in their lively bodies, of the relationships with family and friends, of knowledge and skills and of how to imagine, play, solve problems, and apply formal techniques and rules.

This is clearly an enterprise that fosters moral as well as intellectual and practical learning, and that sees knowing as part of creating, art and technique together. It makes clear why services to children must be integrated, and why professionals at all levels must be prepared to listen to and observe one another, if they are to meet changing and complementary needs in child health and development.

There are chapters on how children learn in embodied movement, in sympathetic communication and in affectionate relationships, as well as on the developing body and its senses. Reference is made to new scientific understanding of the child's brain as a growing organ of imagining and communicating that has sensitive periods and vulnerability at times of fast change, as in toddlerhood when language blossoms. A human brain is knowledge in formation and it has its phases of excitement and adventurous seeking, and periods to gain strength in reflective peace, which may be more fragile. The child has need for special relationships and the pleasure of being somebody who knows the interest and joy of pride in achievement. This, we now begin to see, is because human brains are built to sympathetically reflect intentions and interests and to grow ideas and make memories with communicable emotions. We also know that a lonely, neglected or abused child may suffer lasting damage to the vital core of the brain where motives for living and learning reside. Brains, young or old, like company, as well as time off to experiment and think. None of this brain knowledge can replace sensitive commonsense about children's needs, but we can be glad that there is so much hard evidence now that the brain is much more than an information-processing machine and a receptacle for instruction.

In Craigmillar it is possible to experience a diversity of families and cultures, and to see how this experience may be examined to enrich the children's understanding of the social world, and how it may make family ties strong and rich in art and discovery, as well as give the whole community a stronger identity, while respecting each child, parent or teacher as a person. And I cannot imagine a better way to foster more healthy eating and combat childhood illnesses of civilization, such as obesity and diabetes, than to involve children and adults in cooking classes together, making healthy eating enjoyable joint work, as indeed it usually is in pre-industrial societies.

Play is valued as a complex expression of motives of experiment, to learn, to share and to invent, as well as a way to journey in the historic time of knowledge long long ago, and to imagine new worlds. Books and literacy are keys to the bigger world of the culture's imagination, to be contrasted, I would say, with the junk knowledge of the media, computer games and the information highway of the internet. I am delighted with the emphasis given to dance and experiments with drama, and the use of these to foster both interest in different traditions brought from foreign lands and pride in the rich Scottish tradition. I believe strongly in the basic importance of musicality in communication, in the power of dynamic emotional expression outside language to build bonds of companionship and enhance creative imagination. Clearly Tina Bruce and her Craigmillar partners do, too.

All the wisdom of this experiment in learning how to learn and how to teach by cooperative awareness has application beyond the early years. It can open up primary schools through the catalyst of nursery schools to a more integrated approach. The evidence is clear that un-whole provision (and the factory model) does not benefit the development of self-motivated learning. The value, economic and social, of integrated services in the community is proven. The maintained nursery schools, with trained and qualified staff and early-years teachers, have given over 70 years' service and their worth needs promoting again. They were right to resist 'the trend from the 1970s towards an overemphasis on intellectual development in school settings, or the emphasis on social emotional and physical development in day care settings,' page 6.

The Craigmillar community can be proud, indeed, of the work of their schools and community groups, which can light the way to recovery of a way of learning with children that benefits everyone.

Professor Colwyn Trevarthen

Preface for the 0–8 Series

The 0–8 Series has stood the test of time, maintaining a central place among early childhood texts. Practitioners have appreciated the books because, while very practical, the series presents a holistic approach to work with young children, which values close partnership with families and their communities. It is evidence based, drawing on theory and research in an accessible way.

The 0–8 Series, now being revised and updated, continues to deal with the themes of early childhood which have always been of concern and interest to parents, practitioners and the children themselves. The voice of the child has, since 1989, been under threat in education. Each author has made an important contribution in their field of expertise, using this within a sound background of child development and practical experience with children, families, communities, schools and other early childhood settings. The series consistently gives a central place to the interests and needs of children, emphasizing the relationship between child development and the socio-cultural learning with which biological and brain development is inextricably linked. The voice of the child is once again being understood as being important if children are to develop and learn effectively, and if adults helping them to learn (teaching them) are to be effective in their work.

The basic processes of communication, movement, play, self-esteem and understanding of self and others, as well as the symbolic layerings in development (leading to dances, reading, writing, mathematical and musical notations, drawing, model-making) never cease to fascinate those who love and spend time with children. Some of the books in this series focus on these processes of development and learning, by looking at children and their contexts in a general way, giving examples as they go. Other books take a look at particular aspects of individual children and the community. Some emphasize the importance of rich physical and cultural provision and careful consideration of the environment indoors and outdoors and the way that adults work with children.

As Series Editor I am delighted to reintroduce the 0–8 Series to a new readership. The re-launched series enters a more favourable climate than the original series, which survived (and flourished) in a hostile climate of literacy hours for four-year-olds, adult-led learning, and a lack of valuing diversity, multi-lingualism, imagination and creativity. This revised and updated 0–8 Series will inform, support and inspire the next generation of early childhood practitioners in the important work they do, in a climate which will encourage rather than undermine.

I look forward to seeing the impact of the 0–8 Series on the next decade.

PROFESSOR TINA BRUCE
University of Surrey Roehampton

Background

Holistic services for whole children

There are historic traditions, geographic and cultural factors in developing the learning of young children.

It is not possible to describe in one book the many different ways in which children develop, learn and grow up in different families and in different parts of the world. Nor is it possible to encapsulate the knowledge and understanding of what is involved in children developing learning, which has been built up over time.

The Castlebrae Community Cluster

This book has emerged out of the work I have been privileged to be part of from 1999 to 2003 in the Castlebrae Community Cluster, which is part of the Craigmillar area in Edinburgh. The group comprises:

- The Books for Babies Group (Library and National Literacy Trust)
  Maxine Behan, Teresa Martin, Beth Cross
- Cameron House Nursery School
  Chris McCormick, Anne Chalmers, Maureen Allan, Melanie Dow
- Castlebrae Family Centre, based in the Castlebrae Community High School
  Lyn Tarlton, June Fraser, Anne Kilpatrick
- Children's House Nursery School
  Maureen Baker, Maggie Miedzybrodzka, Margaret Murdoch, Fiona Cropley, Sonia Anderson, Christine Vesco, Theresa Spence, Margaret Grieve, Josie McKeon
- Craigmillar Children and Families Centre
  Liz McCulloch, Rachel Barnes, Gillian Cooper, Margaret Haddow, Kelly

Hastings
- Food for Tot Healthy Eating Project based at Greengables Nursery School
  Christine McKechnie and Barbara Jessop
- Greendykes Children and Families Centre
  Isobel Gunn, Emily Kyle, Helen Sweeney, Linda Finna, Janine Williamson, Anne Milligan, Melody Spinrad, Carol Chalmers, Linda Laidlow
- Greengables Nursery School
  Carol Morley, Mary Brock, Sue Geggie, Linda Jamieson, Lesley Lewis, Joyce Mitchell, Katriona Owens, Sheila Robertson, Sue Waine, Kate Frame, Gitte Reiche, Helga Pinstrup
- Peffermill (now Castleview) Primary School
  Elizabeth Sharp, Kirsty Hastings, Jennifer Graham, Carol Skirving
- Prestonfield Primary School
  Lynda Melvin, Sarah Cook, Muriel Monteith, Katrina Vernon
- Princess Elizabeth Nursery School
  Lucy Fraser Gunn, Joyce Horberry, Julie Bannantyne, Catriona Clarke, Norma Smith
- St Francis Primary School
  Margaret Lamb, Jean Inglis, Sheila Molineux

One of the exciting and challenging aspects of this group beginning to work together through community funding was the impact of the different cultures, traditions and training of the various agencies working with children and families.

The traditions of training for practitioners with health, children's services, voluntary-sector or education backgrounds are varied, and so it is of paramount importance to seek out the shared ground, and not to be halted at the first hurdle by an emphasis on differences of approach and practice. The Castlebrae Community Cluster has made great strides in doing this, but everyone involved is aware that what has been achieved is only the beginning, as the community continues to change.

Shared in-service training

Important shared ground was established through the project we explored together in several in-service training days. We discussed how children become symbol users from babyhood onwards, emphasized the importance of first-hand direct experience, how children represent experience, predict it or rearrange it, the importance of play, and how children learn the culture through the rules and games of the society and people they grow up with.

Follow-up

Intensive follow-up work in each setting, after each in-service day, culminated in a conference at the Castlebrae Community High School in May 2001. The title of the conference was 'The development of symbolic behaviour in early childhood'.

Each setting presented an exhibit showing its work on the project, in video, annotated photographs and artefacts. Parents spoke at the conference. The staff were available to talk to visitors about their work. Local politicians, press, directors of services and other representatives of the Edinburgh Local Authority attended.

The collaboration of the Castlebrae Community Cluster continued to develop, with more in-service training days and smaller sub-group gatherings. I have been the scribe, gathering up the different areas. My enhancement of the text with additional theory and research will form material to which we shall return for further discussions and developments in the work of the Castlebrae Community Cluster.

Nursery schools

Nursery schools came into being because of committed people who wanted to bring integrated services to disadvantaged communities. Sometimes societies and settlements raised the funds for their establishment in communities. Sometimes individuals gave endowments.

In the UK there is a strong tradition of integrated services for whole families and children in the maintained nursery schools, pioneered by the Scottish-born Margaret McMillan at the turn of the twentieth century. They are maintained by the local authorities in whose area they are situated. They have always maintained strong connections with health services, and health visitors and other health professionals often work in them regularly, for instance in clinics. There are agreements with children's services to work with children in need or at risk and with families where children have special educational needs or disabilities. Many are involved in local playgroups, preschools and other voluntary and community groups and services, and are often linked with childminding networks. They have also pioneered and worked for seamless transitions for children, connecting with colleagues in primary schools.

Maintained nursery schools

Maintained nursery schools have emerged from the EPPE research (2002) as the most integrated and deepest, sustained high-quality provision for work with both children and parents. They have highly trained and qualified staff, led by trained early-years head teachers. They are good value for money and responsive to their communities, and are more often than not a one-stop shop for families; 58 percent of them became Early Excellence Centres in England, and many could transform into Children's Centres. They were singled out for praise in David Bell's (Her Majesty's Chief Inspector for England) report (2003) and in the Scottish Commission Reports.

In the Castlebrae Cluster there are four maintained nursery schools, of which three have time-honoured histories (Swanson, 1975).

The Princess Elizabeth Nursery School

This nursery school, founded in 1930, follows a typical path in that it was founded (named the Princess Alice Child Garden) as the direct result of a visit from Margaret McMillan to the Montessori Society (Jamieson, 1975: 32). Nursery schools often became established through funds from societies committed to work with young children. The school is located above a child and family health clinic.

Greengables Nursery School

Following the Head Start Programmes in the United States in the 1960s, some new nursery schools were built, such as Greengables, founded in 1975. These schools reflected the findings of the various studies (Athey, 1990), which pointed to the importance of parental involvement in developing children's learning; and having a curriculum framework which gave children experiences which tapped into their interests, and helped them to develop their ideas, thoughts and creativity, and to express themselves through spoken language and a variety of other media, such as painting, construction, role play, song, dance and movement.

Children's House Nursery School

Children's House was built by an anonymous benefactor, but it has emerged that this was Marjorie Rackstraw. The school, founded in 1935, was selected for a Schools Curriculum Award in 2002.

Cameron House Nursery School

This nursery school was founded in 1934 by a voluntary organization, the University of Edinburgh Settlement, through an endowment from Grace Drysdale. The settlement was part of a movement bringing education to communities overwhelmed by poverty. The school has welcomed prestigious visitors such as Sir James Barrie, King George V and Queen Mary, and Winston Churchill. (Penman, 1975: 31).

 The nursery has stained-glass panels by William Wilson, which tell the story of a day in the life of children at play. If you look above and at the front cover of the book, you will find an example of one of the stained-glass panels.

Nursery schools since 1945

Cameron House and Children's House were typical in being taken over after the Second World War by the local education authority. The emphasis then was on taking mothers away from working for the war effort, and to return them to full-time motherhood. The nursery school tradition in the UK has been eroded by successive governments, who have cut back the health, community, social and family education services, reduced the hours and neglected the buildings.

Those committed to maintained nursery schools have yearned to return to the integrated provision of the early nursery schools. In the UK, where nursery schools have survived, there are signs that this is beginning to happen once again.

Nursery schools continue to develop the whole child and work with parents and various agencies. They resisted the trend from the 1970s towards an over-emphasis on intellectual development in school settings, or the emphasis on social, emotional and physical development in day-care settings.

There is now a reawakened understanding of the contribution of the traditions which remain the battered vision of those working in maintained nursery schools, of an integrated service, which is responsive to the local community, parents and families and offers adult education classes, health-care, family welfare and child education.

In Castlebrae, the nursery schools work closely with the local secondary and primary schools, ensuring a cluster approach to education. Recently, the nursery schools worked with early-years practitioners in the primary schools to produce a cluster approach to early writing, developing a joint paper together. The Cluster Group aims to develop a cohesive and consistent approach from early childhood and throughout the period of children's school. 'Key Principles for Behaviour and Literacy' have also been agreed. There is also a 'Cluster Approach to Learning and Teaching' because these arise as priorities in the Cluster Development Plan.

In addition, health, children's services, voluntary and community workers are all represented in this book, committed to a multi-agency approach and in the projects 'Books for Babies' and 'Food for Tot'.

Books for Babies

The Books for Babies is a project of the Craigmillar Literacy Trust, managed by a multi-professional steering group, including nursery and home link teachers, librarians, health visitors and parent representatives.

When books are enjoyed by both children and adults together, they are one of the most powerful ways in which children join in with their culture in the UK and many other parts of the world. The aims and objectives of the Craigmillar Books for Babies project state:

> *Educational research shows that a child's reading ability is significantly affected by experience prior to formal education. This project directly*

encourages parents and carers to actively involve their children with books at an early age.

Food for Tot project

'From the moment we are born, someone is worrying about how or what to feed us.'

This statement is from the resource pack, funded by Sure Start Edinburgh, supporting the Food for Tot (food for small children) project which has a co-ordinator based at Greengables Nursery School and a development worker. This is a community-based project in the Craigmillar area, which has grown from small beginnings at Greengables Nursery School, encouraged by Carol Morley. The resource pack states:

> *It is based around the belief that eating habits developed in early childhood have a significant effect upon adult health. Therefore making positive changes in the diet of young children can prevent the onset of health problems in later life. Recent research suggests a worrying increase in diseases such as obesity and diabetes. These and other so-called 'Illnesses of Civilisation', previously affecting adults, are now occurring in childhood. These factors, coupled with requests for diet related help and advice from parents attending the cookery group at Greengables, led to the development of 'Food for Tot'.*

Working with community dental educators

The development worker links with local health visitors and community dental educators to develop and deliver sessions to parents and carers in each centre. The courses aim to:

- encourage a balanced diet;
- develop parents' basic dietary knowledge so that they can make positive choices for their families;
- address questions parents may have associated with the diet, health and well-being of their children;
- increase parental confidence and encourage family cohesion;
- develop skills and knowledge that encourage a positive start in young children's lives.

Group members choosing

The sessions are based on the group's requests, and can focus on any of these key issues.

- Diet during pregnancy
- Breast feeing or bottle feeding
- Weaning
- Toddlers
- Family mealtimes
- Nutrition for the family
- Dental health
- Practical skills (including adults and children cooking together)

The group members decide if they want discussion, taster sessions, practical cookery sessions or videos. They include women who are thinking of having a baby, women who are pregnant, new parents, parents of older babies or toddlers, parents of children under three, and carers of babies and children under three.

> *We see this as a positive aspect of this highly successful project which uses a multi-disciplinary approach to work with parents in a community based setting.* (Christine McKechnie and Barbara Jessop)

The children and families centres and the primary schools

Craigmillar and Greendykes, through their participation in the joint in-service training days, and engagement in the follow-up projects and exhibition conference, together with the three primary schools, Peffermill (now Castleview), Prestonfield, and St Francis and the Castlebrae Family Centre in the Community High School, have begun to work more closely through the catalyst of the nursery schools.

A more integrated approach is, albeit slowly, beginning to develop in primary schools, with after-school clubs, breakfast clubs and wrap-around-care, and more involvement with parents.

There is a slow but progressive realization that children and families do not benefit from unwhole provision if they are to develop their learning both broadly and deeply.

1

How does learning develop?

Key themes

This chapter connects with the central themes of developing learning through the senses, movement, communication, spoken and signed languages, relationships, feelings, thoughts and ideas, becoming a symbol user and being a whole person. Developing learning can only occur with other people, but children need personal space as well as companionship. The chapter emphasizes the importance for adults working with young children of understanding about the following:

- Critical and sensitive periods of development
- The senses and feedback from movement
- Communications without words
- Walking, talking and pretending
- Other people's roles

Christopher's mum has wrapped him up warm because it is a cold, raw, wet day. She thought about whether she would go out with her two year old son because of the unpleasant weather, but the thought of seeing Lyn and June at the Family Centre urged her on. Christopher sits quietly, looking around him from under his hood. When he turns his head, one eye goes under the hood. His ability to look has come a long way since he was born, and before he was born.

The basic 'wiring' of the visual system is innate, but the brain needs proper early visual experiences to refine the connections and achieve adult levels of performance. There are two major requirements for proper early visual performance:

- that the eyes form clear images;
- that both eyes are stably aligned so that they are pointed at the same target in space and send nearly identical, non-conflicting images to the brain (Tychsen, 2001: 67).

Christopher has both of the requirements. If he did not, then there would need to be intervention within the first six months of his birth, so that he could see in depth with normal eye tracking and achieve what is called binocular vision (both eyes working together).

Critical periods

Researchers argue about what are (and are not) critical periods in development. The development of binocular vision takes place within a specific time span (the first three months of life) which cannot be missed. It is genuinely a critical period.

Bruer (2001: 4) argues that: 'The core idea is that having a certain kind of experience at one point in development has a profoundly different impact on future behaviours than having that same experience at any other point in development.' Bruer and Symons 2001, p.4

All humans benefit from seeing clearly with binocular vision because it allows them to follow the movements of people and objects, see them in depth and reach out for them. When something, like binocular vision, is important for any human anywhere in the world, despite the diversity of situations in which human beings live, then critical periods are found in relation to that part of developing learning. This is not the case when cultural influences are stronger in their impact on development.

For example, whereas everyone benefits from binocular vision, not everyone needs the same language. Depending on where they grow up and who they meet, they need to be able to relate to different people differently, and to deal with changing cultural contexts. These aspects of development are facilitated by being given windows of opportunity which keep doors open and allow further language learning.

Interestingly, Bruer (in Bruer and Symons, 2001) does not consider the study of the development of sensitive periods in language (Lenneberg, 1967) or relationships (Harlow, 1958) as central to studying the development of the brain: 'we should note that, for the most part, this was behavioural research, not brain science.' (Bruer, 2001: 8)

Meade (2003: 14) suggests that this means that Bruer ignores the development of language, self, knowledge about relationships, and the impact of experience of culture and relationships with other people on the development of the brain

Sensitive periods

Sensitive periods refer to times when, for example, humans learn sitting, walking and talking to become a symbol user.

The same principles apply also to these periods as they do to critical periods, but the window of opportunity lasts longer. Colin Blakemore, in a lecture at the RSA (2001) said that the windows of opportunity during critical and sensitive periods vary in their function. In the case of binocular and depth perception, the window slams shut when the critical period for that development has passed. With sensitive periods, such as the time frame for learning to walk, the window gradually creaks shut over a much longer time, which may be years (see below). This has important implications for those working with young children and their families.

Throughout this book we shall return to the fact that children are biologically driven to develop in certain ways, whether they live in Edinburgh or anywhere else in the world. Gopnik, Meltzoff and Kuhl (1999) suggest that, unless there is a disability or delay in development, it does not matter where children grow up, they are born with the brain potential to:

- study and remember faces;
- use facial expressions to show feelings;
- learn how objects move;
- work out how objects disappear;
- link cause and effect;
- work out how to categorize objects;
- work out how the sounds of language divide;
- link information from the different senses by forming images;
- transform two-dimensional pictures into three-dimensional objects.

However, individual children grow up in individual ways in different families and cultures. Bortfield and Whitehurst (2001: 188) say that: 'If researchers are willing to expand the concept of sensitive periods to include ... culturally framed windows of opportunity for learning, then the implications for early intervention and educational practice will expand tremendously.

Biologists, neuroscientists, cognitive psychologists, anthropologists, social evolutionists and socio-culturalists and with experts in other disciplines, are finding areas where there is converging evidence, and this is enabling practitioners to help young children develop their learning.

Breathing in and smelling life

Christopher smells the wet air around him. Babies have a stronger sense of smell than adults. But adults often remark that a particular smell brings back a childhood memory. Perhaps the smell of the disinfectant in the corridor of the Family Centre in the Community High School his mother attends will bring back memories of his journey to get there, when he is older. It is more likely that the smell of baking, which is a regular activity offered to the parents, babies and toddlers will evoke later memories.

We more easily remember experiences in which we have actively participated and we will look at the importance of memory in the developing brain in Chapter 2. Here we can simply note that smells can evoke pleasant and unpleasant memories. Ratey, a clinical psychiatrist, writes (2001: 62):

Of all the ways of getting sensory information to the brain, the olfactory system is the most ancient and perhaps the least understood ... Smells can have powerful effects. They can frighten us, intrigue us or comfort us. Because the olfactory system in the brain has a short and direct connection to the memory centres, smells can take us right back to a vivid scene from the past. Different people can detect the same odour and come away with vastly divergent experiences.

Moving and learning

Although Christopher is sitting quietly in his push-chair on the journey, a good observer of young children will see that he never stops moving. His hands and fingers are in a constant state of adjustment, as are his feet. His legs and arms move about all the time (Goddard-Blythe, 2000). He smacks his lips.

It is very difficult to learn or think when movement is constrained. Lying down actually causes the brain to slow down and relax.

For young developing brains, such as Christopher's, it is particularly important that he is not in the push-chair for too long, and that he is given as much freedom of movement as possible when he reaches the Family Centre. For young children, freedom of movement means freedom to learn. (Davies, 2003). As Christopher moves, he receives kinaesthetic (physical) feedback to the brain through his body, limbs and head. This kind of feedback is his window on the world and is one of the key ways in which he makes meaning of his experiences and can learn from them.

A world of sound

All around him, the rain is falling. His mum used to draw a plastic cover over him when it rained, but he cried so much that she stopped doing so. Children often know what is good for them. Because his face is to the rain, he smells, can see more clearly, and he can hear the sounds of the rain falling on the pavement, and the sound of the wheels splashing through puddles, and cars swishing along. Life sounds quite different according to the weather.

All the senses interact with each other and work in synchrony. Some people find they cannot hear very well without their glasses, or perhaps they do not like to talk on the telephone because they cannot see the other person's face. Senses do not work in isolation. 'Making' sense involves the different senses working together.

Christopher quite literally tastes the air. He eats it. This is one of the reasons why cigarette smoking is not allowed in the Family Centre.

Young children absorb smoke as if they are consuming it and smoking themselves, with a higher risk of cancer and respiratory and heart conditions. Taste and smell are closely linked.

Ratey (2001: 66) says: 'One study of children who went to schools in areas with persistent air pollution even showed that the scents increase aggression.'

Children growing up in urban and industrial areas often suffer from blocked noses and ears. GPs in London report that children in the first five years have frequent colds and temporary hearing losses because of blocked tubes.

Orr (2003: 57) stresses the importance of learning through the senses and movement for children with complex needs, emphasizing how the sense of smell seems to be particularly important. Perfumes mask the information to the brain about a smell. He stresses that children learn through unpleasant as well as pleasant smells.

The sounds of recognition and arrival

They have arrived. Until now, Christopher's mum has not spoken to him on the journey. But Christopher makes a pleased sound of recognition. He strains forward as if urging the push-chair on. 'Careful Christopher,' she says. 'We're nearly there.' His mum knows that it is important to talk to her son. This is one of the reasons why she enjoys taking him to the Family Centre. It makes it easier to chat to him and the staff and other parents.

Because the push-chair faces forward, it is more difficult to chat to him as they go along (Griffin, 2003: 5). Most push-chairs are designed like this, and are not designed so that the child faces the person pushing. This would help parents and carers to have conversations with the child.

Communication with and without words or signs

As they reach the door, June greets them. There is a smile from Lyn, and Christopher's legs flail about with excitement and pleasure, and he struggles to get out of the push-chair. He is quite literally reaching out to her with his whole self and body.

When we reach out into the world with our bodies, our minds reach out too, and it is the total system, the brain, body and environment, that determines the content of our consciousness ... the environment itself is effectively part of us, almost like an 'add-on' bit of the brain. (Carter, 2002: 183)

Christopher has eye contact with June, and his hands flap with pleasure. His mother undoes the straps, saying, 'Ooh, quick, quick! I know you want to get out!', and he speeds across to the sand tray, where he picks up a small shovel, and collects sand on it, watching where it falls. These are different kinds of non-verbal communication.

'Gestures are an intrinsic part of language, and are not an "add-on".' (Carter, 2002: 194)

Christopher's gestures 'speak' to his mother at once. She understands that he wants to be out of the push-chair and into the sand as soon as can be managed. As she speaks to him she is 'wrapping his gesture with words' (Carter, 2002: 194). She has given him key words that matter in this situation, such as 'quick', and 'out'. Developing concepts about time and space are a crucial part of developing intellectual learning.

- Quick – this is a word about time.
- Out – this is a word about space.

Christopher in the sand with his dinosaur

Walking, talking and pretending

Most children do three extraordinary things in the first two years of their brain development. They begin to talk, walk and pretend (DfES, 2003). These three aspects of development seem to go forward together. Christopher can walk. He has a few words and phrases he can say, and he enjoys story rhymes and simple stories in books, or with puppets and dolls and small-world arti-facts, such as animals, or cars that June has introduced him to with his mum at the Family Centre.

He is beginning to become a symbol user, and make one thing stand for another. The development of learning through the senses and movement helps children develop into becoming a symbol user. Language, pretend play and using symbols are three different ways in which humans make one thing stand for another. The word 'sand' is not the sand. It stands for the sand. We can use the word to describe the sand to Christopher as he uses it, but we can also talk about the sand when it is not there.

When he gets home, his mum might say to him, 'You liked playing with the sand today, didn't you, Christopher?' The word 'sand' has a pleasurable feeling for Christopher. The Latin verb for emotion is *'movere'*. As Carter (2002) says, this means that words really do physically 'move' us. We jump for joy, stamp with anger, for example.

Christopher will have learnt about the materials provided at the Castlebrae Family Centre. He chose to spend time playing with the sand and the small-world dinosaurs. Play is very important in developing learning, and is one of the central ways in which young children learn. It helps them to make sense of material and people and to get the most from interacting with them. It also helps them to move from the immediate to the past and future through the imagination and a world of pretending.

The world of people

Whatever the brain does is triggered by what is out there in the environment. Both people and objects are important when we consider how babies, toddlers and young children develop their learning.

Christopher certainly loved the dinosaurs in the sand, but being with June and Lyn and meeting other children was also central to his sand play. The staff provided the sand and the dinosaurs. His Mum took him to the Castlebrae Family Centre to play with it. The other children were also taken there to play. Adults let him choose to play with the sand. Other children joined him there, and they began to play as companions, to disrupt each other's play, and to be helped to co-operate and enjoy being together with the support of the adults.

The need for companionship

People, babies and adults, need other people. We both influence and are influenced by others in the ways we feel, think, develop ideas, move and relate to people. It is just as important to pay attention to these socio-cultural aspects of development as to study the brain's development.

Who else was there on the day that Christopher and his mum visited the Family Centre? Christopher has been involved in the centre since he was born. Lyn Tarlton, the teacher, writes:

Christopher has been involved in the Craigmillar 'Books for Babies' project since his birth. His family is extremely interested in literacy issues. He frequently has stories read to him, and he is happy to read to himself. He visited Drummond Safari Park as part of a Family Centre outing, and photographs were taken. The photographs were displayed on the wall and he, like several other children attending the Centre, often looked at them. He used them as a book to 'read' his interpretation of the visit.

The need for both personal space and companionship

Everyone of every age needs personal space. Christopher, even though he is only 2 years old, needs time to himself to enjoy books and dwell on memories of the outing. He also enjoys companionship and sharing stories with other children, learning through imitating the things they do and seeing how they use his ideas too. This is communication which is non-verbal. When Christopher and his mum arrived at the Centre, a range of non-communication took place. This included eye contact, facial expressions, smiles, eyes wide open, hand gestures, legs kicking with pleasure and the sound of pleasure. His mum spoke to him in a high-pitched voice, described by Colwyn Trevarthen (1998) as 'motherese', which is talk biologically right for babies and toddlers. This is another kind

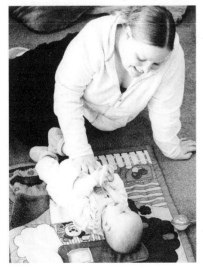

A protoconversation in 'motherese' and movement

In practice

- When you are with young babies and children, do you make sure that you help them to use all their possible senses and movements, so that they can learn effectively? Do you provide a multi-sensory environment?
- Do you follow what they seem to be looking at, and talk around what interests them to look at?
- Do you show them things and point to things you think they might find interesting?
- Do you help them to listen to birds, traffic? Does a bike make the same sound as a lorry? Rain? On the road, or on a bus-shelter roof? A knife scraping on a plate, or the sound of footsteps?
- Do you help children to taste, smell and talk about bitterness, sweetness, sourness and saltiness? Smells, perfume, the scent of flowers, dirt and rubbish, mildew and decomposing, autumn leaves, compost and fertilizers, earth and grass?
- Do you encourage them to touch, hold, manipulate things? Do you help them to hold delicate objects with a fine touch, and have a firm hand when kneading dough?
- Do you give children ample opportunities to use their movements for learning? How free are they to move about indoors and outdoors?
- Fine motor movements develop better when larger movement is encouraged. Remember, children cannot learn much when they are sitting still.
- Do you talk with children, or at them? Talking with children means you listen to what they say and reply to that, or you say things to them which they engage with and want to continue talking about.
- Do you get down to eye level when you engage in conversations with children?
- When you set up the indoor and outdoor areas, do you get down low and see it from a child's point of view?

of non-verbal communication, based on the pitch, rhythm and tempo of the sounds.

Although these kinds of non-verbal communication are central, talking and signing are also very important. This is because talking or signing allows children to make a quantum leap forward in the way they can think beyond the here and now. Words will gradually:

- lead Christopher into abstract, flexible, imaginative, innovative thinking;
- enable him to think from different points of view, which helps in relating to people;
- help him to develop self discipline;
- help him to understand how he feels;
- help him to manage his feelings.

Further reading

Bruce, T. and Meggitt, C. (2002) *Childcare and Education*, 3rd edn. London: Hodder and Stoughton.

Carter, R. (1998) *Mapping the Mind*. London: Seven Dials.

Gopnik, A., Meltzoff, A. and Kuhl, P. (1999) *How Babies Think*. London: Weidenfeld and Nicolson.

Makin, L. and Spedding, S. (2002) 'Supporting Parents of Infants and Toddlers as First Literacy Educators: an Australian Initiative', *Early Childhood Practice: The Journal for Multi-Professional Partnerships* 4(1): 17–27.

Meade, A. (2003) 'What Are the Implications of Brain Studies on Early Childhood Education?', *Early Childhood Practice: the Journal for Multi-Professional Partnerships* 5(2): 5–19.

2

Mind and brain

Key themes

In this chapter we look at the long journey that has been made in the development of the brain. We consider how the brain works and how it learns. The brain:

- makes connections;
- prunes itself when parts are not used;
- lays down memories;
- has chemicals called neuro-transmitters which cause a state of heightened alert when fear or danger are sensed and open us up to learning when we are in a state of well-being;
- is able to consciously scrutinize itself;
- can get inside the heads, feelings and motivation of others through developing consciousness.

Learning to talk and becoming a symbol user develops consciousness, and requires a long childhood. The periods of the greatest development of an area of the brain are also the periods of the greatest vulnerability. If adults help children to learn through their interests and meet their needs through these, then the children will open up to learning.

It is unusual to find books and articles which look at both the mind and the development of the brain together. Carter (1998, 2002) has done so in a reader-friendly way in her books about the brain and consciousness. The two go together, but it is easier to understand the workings of Christopher's nervous system and physical aspects of his brain than it is the workings of his mind. Considering the two together helps us to make sense of what is important in

Christopher's development, and to bear in mind that he is a whole person.

The brain has taken millions of years to evolve into its present-day form, and it is still evolving. It has added layers as it has become more sophisticated. Its adult form is too big for mothers to give birth, and so babies are born with incomplete brains which continue to develop after birth. This is why babies and toddlers are so dependent and attached to people.

The brain continues to develop and change throughout our lives, because we are creatures capable of constant learning, which means adapting, modifying and being sufficiently flexible to try new things, using what we know in new ways. We saw that Christopher was not born with binocular vision. His brain developed the possibility for it, and the way it developed was shaped by experience. Nurture shapes nature (Blakemore, 2001).

Christopher's brain

Meade (2003) explains that the 100 billion brain cells called neurons are formed at birth, and they are in the right locations, 'but most are not connected, nor are they mature'. Binocular vision develops in the first two months, but other parts of the brain develop on different time scales. Christopher's movement has yet to develop hopping and skipping, although he can walk, run and jump. He can co-ordinate sounds enough to make sense of language sounds, and to speak in phrases and simple sentences.

The brain is part of the central nervous system. The other parts of the nervous system are the spinal cord and the peripheral system (which include the sensory nerves for input and motor nerves for acting out what the brain says). The central nervous system has a genetically programmed sequence of development. Put simply, it develops from, 'tail to head'. The top of the head, the cerebral cortex region of the brain, develops last. (Meade, 2003: 6)

The oldest part of the brain in evolution

Christopher's brain stem cells deal with his breathing, blood pressure and heart beat, sending messages through the nerves of his spinal column. This is what is sometimes called his instinctive or reptilian brain. It takes over from the parts of the brain which evolve later, when survival, fear and threat are sensed.

Christopher's cerebellum, which is also connected to his brain stem, probably developed during the period of evolution when mammals evolved. It

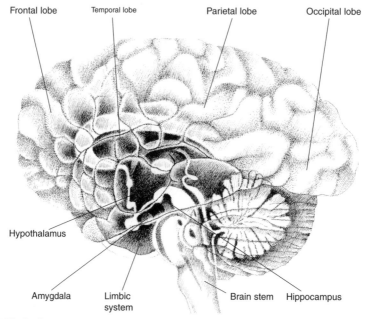

Figure 2.1 The brain

deals with the co-ordination of movement. This is sometimes called the mid-brain, or the mammalian or limbic system. It is the centre of Christopher's emotional life. This area of his brain also deals with long-term memory. Its Latin name is hippocampus.

The amygdala filters information coming into the brain through the senses, which relate to matters of survival and emotion. Both the hippocampus and the amygdala convert short-term memory into long-term memory. They are connected to most areas of the brain, because survival issues and feelings evoked in emergencies are essential.

Other areas of the brain, which deal with feeling safe or fearful, are the thalamus and the hypothalamus. These take in outside information through the senses, and relay them to the relevant parts of the brain.

From this description we can see that human feelings have evolved so that Christopher can react to events quickly, be safe and survive. We shall see below that attachment to loved and important people is an important way in which this is achieved. Feelings also help Christopher to keep hold of memories, and make meaning of them by linking them to how he felt when events were experienced. It is easier for Christopher to lay down long-term memories that have engaged him emotionally. We are more likely to forget

experiences that we do not have deep feelings about. We can see how important Christopher's attachment and love for his mum is, and how he enjoys
seeing June and Lyn. He wants to share books, dinosaurs and sand play with
them and this helps him to be adventurous by beginning to play with other
children under their protection and with their help.

The most recent part of the brain in evolution

Human brains are, more than other animals, capable of flexible thinking. This
is because the human brain has evolved so that three-quarters of the cortex is
committed to flexible thinking. Its surface looks a bit like the crinkly bark of
a tree, and it is divided into two hemispheres. The two sides are connected
and depend on each other, behaving for most of the time as if they are one.
This is important to bear in mind, because sometimes the differences between
the two parts is over-emphasized, instead of the co-ordinated features.

Just as it is inaccurate to suggest that the two hemispheres of Christopher's
brain have specific functions, so it is not true to say that the four lobes of his
cerebrum have specific jobs to do, but they do exert particular general influences on behaviour. Neuroscientists such as Blakemore (2001) and Susan
Greenfield (2000) do not see the lobes as having any connection with what
different parts of the anatomy do.

The occipital lobe is primarily concerned with the processing of vision. The
parietal lobe mainly influences movement, orientation and number calcula-
tions. The temporal lobes exert influence over hearing (sounds) and language
(understanding) and some aspects of memory. The frontal lobes influence
conscious understanding of mood, emotions, and higher-order thinking
such as planning, making decisions, having a vision of what to aim for and
concepts. This is the newest part of the brain in terms of evolution, and does
not fully develop until the twenties.

Electrical signals carrying information to Christopher's muscles or
thoughts are sent through the neurons. These connect at the synapses, which
are like junctions. The axial tips send electric impulses across the synapse and
the dendrites receive them. They are transmitted from the axon to the den-
drite by chemical neuro-transmitters. In this way Christopher's synapses
either excite or inhibit parts of the brain.

When neurons which are near each other consistently fire signals together,
memories are set down. The saying goes that cells that fire together, wire
together, making what Carter (1998) calls the fire dance. The circuits (fire

dance patterns) for Christopher's senses (hearing, vision, touching, tasting, smelling and kinaesthetic) are localized. We may indeed say that Christopher's brain is a chemical-electric miracle (Rowland, 2002, personal communication).

Brain connections in the first three years

Christopher's brain began to form synapses (connections) when his mum was pregnant. By the time he is three years old, his brain will have formed 100 percent more synapses than will be present in his adult brain. (Babies lose the ability see sounds, described as synaesthesia.) This proliferation of synapses forming connections allows great flexibility in the brain as it develops, so that it can be sensitive and adaptive to the environment, experience and context.

Although nature allows for the loss of many of these synapses as part of healthy development, there is also an element of 'use it or lose it'. This allows him to be adaptable, flexible, imaginative and creative, capable of responding to events and ideas in a fast-changing world, and of forming his own ideas to deal with this, participate and contribute.

Christopher and his mum attend the Castlebrae Family Centre, where they sing and dance, play with materials such as sand and water, bake together and chat about what they are doing, and when they get home, remember what they did together. In this way the synapses for language, flexibility through play, and learning through the senses and movement are strengthened and laid down as episodic memories which become a resource Christopher's brain can use later. (See also Chapter 3)

Alongside the sculpting (or pruning) of the synapses in Christopher's brain, the process of myelination takes place. Fat surrounds and insulates Christopher's axons, so that connections do not send faulty signals and are sent more quickly. Axons send signals from the cell nucleus, whilst dendrites receive incoming information. As myelination develops, the flexibility of his brain becomes less. This is why the first years are so important. The richer the first-hand direct experiences he has and the quality of experiences he has with people the more he will be able to develop the possibilities of his brain.

Sensory cells are said to be 'plastic' for a period after they arrive – they can change their function. When neurons become hooked up to each other and wrapped by myelin they lose much (but not all) of their plasticity. Migration to a specific location and layer in the cerebral cortex has significance for defining their functions. (Meade, 2003: 4)

Neuro-transmitters

It is important to realize that the quality of experiences Christopher has will influence the way that chemicals working in different parts of the brain, known as neuro-transmitters, open up or close down his learning. Looked at from one perspective, Christopher's feelings are chemical. Looked at another way, his feelings drive the chemistry that makes his brain function.

It will not be possible for Christopher to learn well if the chemistry is wrong for it. If he feels panic or fear, this will cause his brain to produce the chemical endomorphins, which will close down his learning and take him into survival, fight or flight mode. When he is enjoying playing in the sand, or sharing the 'Thomas and the Dinosaur' story, his brain releases the chemical serotonin (sometimes called the 'feel-good' chemical), which opens him up to new learning, and also helps him to apply what he already knows.

Consciousness

So far, we have concentrated on the physical aspects of Christopher's brain more than his mind. Much of the workings of his brain are at an unconscious level, but Greenfield (2000: 198) says:

> The human brain is an incredible organ. Somehow it generates emotion, language, memories and consciousness. It gives us the power of reason, creativity, intuition. It is the only biological organ able to scrutinise itself and ponder on its inner workings – yet, despite its best effort, those inner workings remain shrouded in mystery.
>
> Collectively, human brains have it in our power to create a world that celebrates our individuality and the diversity of human nature, or to condemn ourselves to a living hell of uniformity and greater standardisation both of nature and nurture. Even if free will is a neuronal sleight of hand – the choice really is our own.

Being conscious of something compared with the state of consciousness

It is important to remember that if Christopher were to be conscious of something, he would be aware of it. This is very different from a state of consciousness. Christopher's brain has yet to develop to a point where he can be in a state of consciousness, because he is still establishing a sense of self (or a sense of identity). We will be looking at this in more detail and consider the implications for developing learning in young children (see Chapter 3).

What is a state of consciousness?

Where is consciousness located?

Carter (2002: 115) suggests that the location of consciousness may be in the limbic system at the place where the parietal and temporal junction lies. This is where Christopher's brain stores his map of self and judges his relationship of himself with the world. There are good connections to the frontal lobes of his cortex, and this bit of his brain can pull in information from the senses.

A sense of embodiment, through the senses, movement and feedback

Christopher, as he learns through his senses and movements, is quite literally developing a sense of self. The temporal lobe stores Christopher's personal memories. The intimate moments he spent showing June the book that his mother gave him involves touch, smell, tasting the smell of the book and June, looking with a shared focus and listening to what June reads and says (sounds). He is using all his senses and movement.

Language as a scaffold to support consciousness

The temporal lobe also processes sounds. 'Language may be the scaffolding that supports consciousness' (Carter, 2002: 115). The left hemisphere is used for language in most people, to describe and tell stories, which are powerful ways in which we become fully conscious.

Spatial memories as a support

The cortex is active in developing spatial memories, body awareness, visual consciousness, rehearsing movements in the mind before actually moving, and in raising our feelings to a conscious level.

The brain as co-ordinator

All of these aspects will come together to give Christopher a conscious sense of self. According to Carter (2002: 245), Christopher is developing a boundary around himself which incorporates things and people beyond his body, but is firm enough to enable him to have a point of view.

Christopher's developing conscious self will give a sense of agency going beyond his physical self. In order to be conscious that he is Christopher (Davies, 2003: 74–5) and his mum is someone else, he needs a sense of unity and continuity. Wherever he goes, he is still Christopher with a:

- boundary around self
- sense of agency
- sense of unity

We need to add Christopher's:

- hopes
- dreams
- beliefs
- social relationships

'All of this is produced by shifting, sparking, fizzing, discontinuous neural firing patterns in our brains' Carter (1998: 245).

Development

Why we need a long childhood

In evolutionary terms, the shorter the childhood, the less flexible the brain can be. A blackbird, for instance, which matures in a matter of weeks, is only capable of singing one tune, with slight regional variations.

Christopher can already sing several songs, and speak as well. Human brains are capable of immense flexibility. Piaget (1947) was one of the first theoreticians to challenge the notion that human intelligence is entirely inherited and fixed at birth. He saw intelligence as adaptation to the experiences of life. Adaptive intelligence means that we can be responsive to people and events and think flexibly according to situations, using past experience to guide us.

Children spend their childhoods:

- attaching themselves to other people, and keeping safe in doing so;
- learning to belong to their community as social beings. Christopher already knows what it is to love his mum;
- developing memories which will act as a resource for the present and for future planning;

- communicating through gesture, facial expressions and without words;
- developing (usually) at least one language and other symbols through which to share, exchange, explain, represent, imagine, create, change, discard ideas through thinking flexibly and learning to understand how they feel, and how to face and deal with their feelings without hurting or destroying;
- playing, which is a powerful mechanism for experimenting with life, physically and imaginatively.

Safe boundaries

Meeting two-year-old Christopher and his mum makes us aware of how fascinating young children are. The word 'learn' is often used as if it is mainly about the thinking and ideas that children acquire. However, children also need to feel safe and secure, with clear boundaries, and to be given warmth and affection if they are to develop, learn and flourish. Children also learn how to know, face and deal with their feelings, the relationships they have with those they love, those they become friends with and those they meet more formally. Children learn how to manage their bodies and movements.

The combination of these things leads to the development of learning. This book is about whole children, and the way that adults who love them and work with them need to develop learning carefully, so that children fully participate in the life of their family and community.

Development is a big word, which holds in it the progress an individual child like Christopher (or an adult) makes in understanding, thinking, relating, feeling, physically moving and feeling feelings, facing feelings and dealing with feelings. It carries a sense of direction that is broad and general rather than narrow and specific. It is a word that empowers a person to be able to keep adjusting and responding to the experiences of life. Development is at the heart of living. It happens spontaneously, unnoticed by those who do not look for it. It has two strands: biological-evolutionary; and socio-cultural.

The brain (the biological and evolutionary side of development) is nothing on its own. It cannot develop without other people. Development through people means learning to be part of family and cultures as well as the world beyond. Experience through people, places, things and cultural events triggers brain development. The brain is shaped and changes through the people we meet and the places we are in, and it has built into it the possibilities to develop relationships with people (Trevarthen,1998).

Learning

Learning deepens where there is care and nurture of the learner; the word means different things to different people.

An approach which emphasizes learning outcomes and targets sees the products of learning as more important than the journey towards knowing and understanding, neither understands feelings and relationships, nor considers the cultural context as central to the intellectual life of a child. In this book another view of learning is taken in which the processes of learning and the dispositions for learning are emphasized (Katz and Chard (1989), Laevers (1994), Pascal and Bertram (1999)). Carr (1999: 81) picks out five dispositions which encourage learning, understanding and knowing things: courage, trust, perseverance, confidence and responsibility. The importance of adults tuning into the inner motivation of the child is stressed. However, the view of learning in this book does not favour the processes of learning more than the learning that takes place. Both the process and the product are important in developing learning. Bruner (1977) believes that when we help children to learn we must make sure the processes of learning are given a great deal of attention. He also thinks that the journey should lead somewhere.

Converging evidence about developing learning

Converging evidence from neuroscience, cognitive psychology, socio-cultural research and anthropology suggests that it is helpful to a child's learning to emphasize learning through direct experiences (the senses and movement) and encouraging a love of narrative and story through books, enjoying being read stories, and understanding what stories are by acting them out, making them up in play scenarios, through role play and the world of pretence, and looking things up (e.g. looking up spiders in a non-fiction book when one has been found in the garden).

Children develop and learn better when both their interests and needs are met (EPPE, 2002). Because we think that children ought to learn something, it does not mean that we can make them learn it. Christopher, having played with the sand for a bit, goes to the push-chair and takes out of the bag hanging from it his new book *Thomas and the Dinosaurs*. He says:

> *'Read it, read it, read it – It's my new book!' From the beginning, there grew a major interest amongst all the children, younger and older. We began by providing a setting for the model dinosaurs, posters and books. Christopher can*

be seen enjoying a reference book on his mother's knee. This led to her buying dinosaur toys and books as Christmas presents for him. (Tarlton, 2002)

Christopher is already developing literacy and the disposition to read and become a bookworm. Because June observes and tunes into Christopher's interests, she is able to meet his learning needs. Providing this is not damaged he should become a lifelong learner.

Periods of great development as periods of great vulnerability

We need a note of caution here. The neuroscientist Colin Blakemore (2001) says that periods of development are also periods of vulnerability. If adults were to try to turn Christopher's pleasure in books into a formal lesson, the chances are he would resist. It is one thing for Christopher to choose to share a book with June, but it is quite different should she decide that he must look at a book with her. That is why the processes of learning need as much attention as what is being learnt.

Adults need to respect biological developments, alongside:

- *supporting the child's interests;*
- *extending the child's interests into deeper, wider and consolidated learning, with a small amount of new learning;*
- *using this to plan what that child needs to involve them in participation in their culture and society and the wider world.*

This approach is in tune with the curriculum framework documents in the four countries of the UK, in the New Zealand curriculum document, *Te Whariki*, and with curriculum approaches in other countries, such as Reggio Emilia, Pistoia in Italy, or the Nordic countries, Finland, Iceland, Norway, Sweden and Denmark.

Developing learning through a child's interests and needs

Christopher and his friends at the Castlebrae Family Centre are interested in dinosaurs. They are a long way from understanding them in the way that Charles Darwin did, but Simone and Bradley are showing an interest in whether or not dinosaurs bite. They found the pictures of the models on the poster on the wall, and then began a period of intense dramatic play with the dinosaurs. The staff have noticed they are interested. They talk to the children about dinosaurs and have provided small-world play props and books.

Being educated while being carefully nurtured suggests an emotional commitment to the child. Relationships are respectful, health and nutrition are nurtured, and attention is paid to fatigue. Feelings matter. This means that attachment and dependency are important (Elfer, 1996: Buckingham and Freud, 1942; Manning-Morton and Thorp, 2003; Forbes, forthcoming). There is a concern for well-being, for being secure, wanted, valued, and that you matter to at least one person. June and Lyn focus on Christopher's intellectual life and his fascination with dinosaurs.

In practice

- Do you give babies and toddlers enough time to manipulate, explore, discover materials like paint, dough, sand, water, grass, and to push and pull objects? Young children should not be rushed to learn.
- Do you provide a calm, warm, affectionate atmosphere, in which children feel free to try things out, supported with a few considered and consistent boundaries to support their well-being?
- Do you talk too much? Talking at children makes them switch off and stop listening. Children appreciate it when you give them words they can use later, so they need what you say to clarify and help them to do this.
- Do you help children to understand how other people feel physically or emotionally, and how different people think? Talking about situations in non-judgemental ways helps this lifelong process.
- Do you encourage children to pretend, and imagine how teddy or a doll feels and thinks? Do you help them to pretend through small-world work?
- Do you introduce them to literature which supports them in beginning to look at how other people might feel and think differently?

Further reading

Carter, R. (2002) *Consciousness*. London: Weidenfeld and Nicolson.

David, T., Gooch, K., Powell, S. and Abbott, L. (2002) 'Review of the Literature to Support Birth to Three Matters: A Framework to Support Children in Their Earliest Years'. DFES/Sure Start.

Griffin, S. (2003) 'Selecting a Pram Which Encourages Communication Between Adults, Babies and Toddlers', *Early Childhood Practice: The Journal for Multi-Professional Partnerships* 5(1): 5–7.

Murray, L. and Andrews, L. (2000) *The Social Baby*. Richmond: CP Publishing.

3

A sense of self

Key themes

Biological-evolutionary and socio-cultural aspects of developing learning mingle, resonate and change each other through constant interaction.
   Early bonding relationships start children off with secure foundations which help them to withstand the challenges of life.
   Children develop their learning with increasing consciousness of themselves through a process of embodiment, attachment to a small number of key people, and by a journey which takes them to the inside of how others will act, feel and think. This enables them to further deepen their ideas and thoughts, together with others and as individual people.

It takes about three years from birth for children to develop consciousness, or the state, described by Carter (2002: 9), who said that consciousness is the '"lights-on" state in which we are aware of our surroundings and aware that we are aware of them'. Consciousness is to do with Christopher becoming aware of himself as a thinking, feeling person. It is usually described as developing a sense of self or sense of identity. It involves body awareness (a sense of embodiment) and being able to think about your own thoughts (metacognition).

A sense of embodiment – knowing I am me

Body image, self-esteem and self-confidence are all part and parcel of the developing understanding and knowledge of self.
   Carter (2002: 8) reminds us that: 'The brain and the body are not separate either – the brain extends its tentacles to the tip of your toes and the body owns the brain as much as the brain owns the body.'

Mind, body and soul – all go together

It is important for children to feel comfortable inside their own bodies. Self-esteem is deeply intertwined with self-image. We say things like, 'I don't feel like myself today.' We quite literally have a physical 'sense' of self. Davies (2003: 1) stresses the importance of developing confident body movements in establishing self-confidence: 'Because movement of young children is seen to be a part and parcel of their everyday lives, the danger is that it can be taken for granted and overlooked in terms of its importance in the educational spectrum.'

The children at Cameron House are encouraged to find out who they are, and to develop a strong self-image and self-esteem. This is particularly crucial between the ages of three and five, because self-identity is only just established and newly emerging states of development are always very vulnerable.

At Cameron House, Maria has many opportunities to develop her physical learning, and so to have a strong sense of embodiment as part of self, body image and good self-esteem. In this way she is helped to become a confident learner, with a strong sense of who she is.

This physical knowledge of herself (embodiment), is part of what is involved as she begins to understand that 'I am me, and that is how I am'. As she moves about in space she:

- creates boundaries around herself in space;
- begins to realize that 'I' am having an experience. 'I' am moving;
- develops a sense of agency, understanding that 'I' can climb and do things;
- begins to realize that 'I' am me both of the moment and over time (a sense of unity).

Giving children practical support

In practical ways this learning is helped by flexible and changeable climbing equipment and slides. The nesting frames enable the equipment to be set up in many different ways. This means that once children are confident with one configuration, they can be challenged with a new layout, and their learning can be extended.

But when children need to consolidate through becoming familiar with the same equipment layout, and to work out what repeatedly brings success, then this also is possible. Because the staff are good observers, they can tune into the needs of children with good effect.

Knowing you are you

A group of children (between three and five years of age) play on the slide in the garden. Maria is becoming more and more confident in her movements, through developing her learning in the garden, and finding out how to balance and feel comfortable inside her body, (Biddulph, 1997). She feels she can now manage being part of a group of children, and no longer needs to be with an adult when she uses the slide.

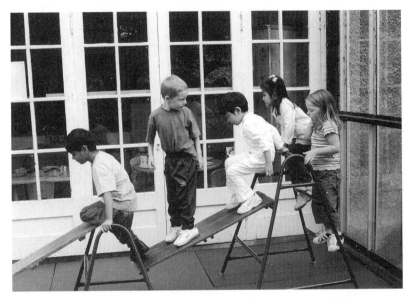

Developing a strong sense of myself and what I can do

However, she is quite anxious about whether she can stay balanced without falling off the climbing equipment when someone is both in front of her as well as close behind her in the processing across the planks and nesting frames. So she sits in a hesitant way, waiting for the boy in front to move forward on to the slide. The boy turns to check that she is all right, sensing that his friend is nervous. Once the plank is clear, she walks in a wobbling way, which certainly does not exude confidence in her body to perform this self-initiated challenge to herself with confidence and ease. Once at the other end of the plank, she turns to check that the girl behind her is not too close to her. She gives her eye contact, and Maria is reassured.

She manages to negotiate going down the slide with no hands, although her body is tense as she does so. At the bottom, she smiles and goes back for another attempt. She is pleased with her physical body. She feels good about herself and her achievement in co-ordinating her body, overcoming her anxiety about whether she can do it, and that she did it in company, receiving the warmth of her companions supporting her through something they knew was not easy for her.

Who am I in time and space, and why do things happen as they do?

We need to keep returning to three other aspects of experience which help children to relate to the question: who am I? This is important, because knowing yourself helps you to learn.

- Who am I in time (past, present and future)?
- Who am I in space?
- Reasons for things happening to me (cause and effect).

These three factors are central to the development of learning, from the beginning of our lives and throughout our lives. Scientists (Carter, 2002) know that even before we have a thought to reach for something, our brain begins to prepare to make the necessary movements. The timing and spatial understanding together with reasoning are in our bodies before they come into our conscious minds. This directs us to reflect on what we mean when we ask, who am I? And who are you?

Developing a point of view

Children who develop a strong, positive sense of themselves, as Erikson (in Bruce and Meggitt, 2002: 160; Erikson, 1963: 264) pointed out in the 1950s, acquire a sense of trust and are optimistic and hopeful about life. They do not develop self-doubt. They are autonomous and able to show initiative. By being located in self children begin quite literally to be able to have a point of view (Carter, 2002: 221).

Cross-cultural diversities

We need to avoid being mono-cultural. The Western world tends to see self more individually than other parts of the world, where self is more linked to being part of a group. However, a group self is present when singing in a choir, dancing in a group, or in a crowd, like when more than a million people marched against the war in Iraq in London in 2003.

Children with complex needs

Some children have some combination of significant motor, sensory, language communication, learning delay. When this is so, they are said to have complex needs. They may have frequent stays in hospital, need nursing at home and require technological support. They may have a life-limiting condition.

Lilli Nielsen's work with children who have complex needs shows us how important the sense of self is. She describes a blind two-year-old boy who although he could sit unsupported and could walk if someone held his hand, never initiated walking by himself. He would sit, tapping his chin.

> *During my first interaction with him, I succeeded in interrupting his stereo-typed behaviour and gaining his interest in objects. This incident was analysed in order to recognise what it was that had changed his pattern of behaviour.*
>
> *So it became clear that although the boy had been moved around, firstly by being carried and later on by walking, hand held, he had no knowledge about spatial relations. He had no knowledge about his surroundings resulting from his own activity. His innate need for activity had resulted in stereotyped activity with his own body.* (Nielsen, 1992: 51)

Children who are not challenged with sensory disabilities, physically or intellectually develop spatial relationships quite naturally, through their daily experiences. They begin to reach for objects intentionally, and as they do so they experience kinaesthetic feedback. Orr (2003: 50) gives an example of David, a child with complex needs, being given the choice of a police-man's hat or a milkman's peaked hat. He says:

> *I had been hoping for the postman's story as I liked the bit where he got chased by a dog. I pondered how I could ask for one that wasn't on offer, whose hat was still in the box on the settee in the little bay window. I twisted my head*

and trunk towards the general direction where I thought they were. ... She observed my movements, saying, 'So you don't want either of those?' which I thought was pretty good (Orr, 2003: 50).

When children are able to sit, they learn to keep their midline so that they do not topple over as they reach for people and objects (Mandler, 1999). David has to develop other strategies to reach for objects he wants to hold.

The views of Nielsen and Orr are linked to Davies's observation:

The indivisibility of movement from human functioning may be one of the reasons why its importance in terms of child development is not always given the serious recognition it deserves. It is so inbuilt that it is not until movement is seen to be dysfunctional or ineffective in some way, such as in autism, depression, attention deficit hyperactive disorder, cerebral palsy or mood swings, that it emerges as a significant educational phenomenon. (Davies, 2003: 1)

Orr points out that if people keep talking to children with complex needs as they interact with objects and try to work out how their bodies and things behave in a world of space, then the children experience difficulties. It is like trying to write an assignment when people keep talking to you. The same is true for babies and toddlers. Knowing when to talk to children, and when to be with them, interested but quietly so, takes skill and sensitivity on the part of the adult.

Nielsen, with the 'Little Room' for children with visual and complex needs and Goldschmied (Goldschmied and Jackson, 1994) with the treasure baskets for sitting babies agree that it is important to give opportunities to explore space and objects without interference.

The Little Room

For the blind child, understanding of position is knowledge about which kind of movement and in which direction in relation to himself the movement must be performed in order to reach the goal. Thus, it is of importance that the 'Little Room' as well as other surroundings are arranged so that the child can learn that a certain movement leads to a certain tactile or auditory experience, that different ways of grasping can lead to contact with the same object, that

use various muscle strength while handling a certain object can lead to pro-
duction of different sounds. (Nielsen, 1992: 60)

The Little Room is constructed according to the child's needs. It is a more
refined version of the commercially manufactured baby frames that can be
bought in the high street. It might be enjoyable and helpful to make a 'Little
Room' designed specifically for developing the learning of lying babies.
Forbes (forthcoming) writes about the importance of observing babies as
they play, and giving them materials informed by these observations. There
are powerful links between the way that Nielsen introduces children with
complex needs to the Little Room and treasure baskets and the way in which
they are offered to sitting babies. When children's individual needs are met,
no matter what their age is, both those with special needs and others
benefit. This is what is meant when we talk of using inclusive principles in
the way we work. Very often what is good for a child with special needs (the
Little Room) is also good for all. Most babies benefit from Little Room types
of experience.

In the individually prepared Little Room objects can be hung from above or
attached to the walls. The principles of choosing the objects are that they should:

- be of pleasure for the child;
- be graspable;
- have tactile and auditory qualities;
- vary in weight and temperature;
- take into account the senses of smell and taste;
- be visually inspiring;
- inspire to play counting games;
- be changeable in shape;
- be comparable, as well as
- be present in such quantities that the child has opportunity
  - to choose
  - to combine experiences
  - to play various sequence games.

(Nielsen, 1992: 72)

Before offering the child their first stay in the Little Room make sure that the
objects placed in it are based on observation of the child's interests and not
just what he/she is thought to need.

The treasure basket

The aim of Goldschmied's treasure baskets is to encourage sitting babies to find out about objects in space, so that they can concentrate and enjoy this demanding activity. However, again in the spirit of inclusion, treasure baskets offer beneficial experiences to older children with complex needs, provided they are presented in age appropriate ways.

> *Perhaps one of the things which an adult may find difficult to do at first is not to intervene, but to stay quiet and attentive. If we think for a moment how we feel when concentrating on some enjoyable but demanding activity, we do not want or need someone constantly to suggest, advise and praise our efforts, we just want to get on with it, though we may be glad to have their friendly company. In this respect, babies are not so different from grownups.* (Goldschmied and Jackson, 1994: 91)

Goldschmied suggests that babies who can sit but not crawl will benefit from the treasure basket, which should contain:

- a wide range of interesting objects;
- which stimulate their developing senses and understanding;
- made of natural (not plastic materials);
- with adult providing security by attentive, but not active, presence.
(Goldschmied and Jackson, 1994: 97)

Resilient children

During the Second World War Anna Freud (Burlingham and Freud, 1942) worked with children and mothers who either were evacuated from London to the country or remained in London during the Blitz. She found that the children were not emotionally damaged even when they experienced bomb explosions and the loss of their homes and constant moves, if they were with their mothers. It was the separation from their loved ones which caused deep distress, even though they were in the physically safer environment of the country. Their distress was ameliorated if they were with brothers or sisters.

It is very important that we have people in our lives to whom we mean a lot, and who love and value us unconditionally. But not every child will experience this within their family. Rather than focus entirely on the pessimistic picture and outlook that this paints for these children, it is much more helpful to emphasize how we can help children to lead full lives emotionally, socially and intellectually even if their lives are far from ideal.

This is the approach taken in the document 'Birth to Three Matters' (David et al., 2002) which picks out these two quotations with central messages from research on the subject, for example:

> *(Early) … experiences represent no more than a first step in an ongoing life path which may be straight or winding, incremental or decremental, depending on the two-way relationship between individuals and their contexts.* (Clarke and Clarke, 2000: 105)

> *Life transitions have to be considered as end products of past processes and as instigators of future ones.* (Rutter, 1989: 46)

Research suggests that early disadvantages can be overcome through the influence of a key person, teacher or friends, who have very positive effects on a child facing challenges in other parts of their lives (see also p. 70).

> *The common strand found by the researchers seems to point to the need for each child to have, from early in their lives, at least one person with whom they have a strong and meaningful attachment relationship, that they 'matter' and that what they do 'matters' to someone. A further important ingredient may be having a strong sense of self, a self who achieves goals and of whom one can be proud.* (David et al., 2002: 38)

Attachments and a secure base

Attachment theory

This has developed from the work of John Bowlby in the 1950s. Holmes (1993: 202–3) writes, 'New family patterns, unimagined by Bowlby, are emerging'. Nevertheless, the fundamental principles of Bowlby's work remain helpful.

- That parents need security themselves if they are to provide it for their children.
- That separation from someone significant is a threat to security in the child and often causes rage and destruction, numb despair and denial before there is reconciliation to it.

- The world must be patterned by the child into some meaningful shape at all costs.
- The child will guard the sense of security he/she has.
- Loss is not seen by the child to be total or arbitrary, but as recoverable.
- The world may be seen in distorted ways in achieving this sense of recovery.
- In the Darwinian sense, people have survived and evolved because they can bond with others, give each other support and communicate together.
- All human beings share the need for a sense of security.

We need to bear in mind that although children everywhere are naturally primed to attachment behaviour, it emerges in very diverse ways in different cultures.

Having a secure base

The early work of Mary Ainsworth (1969), building on Bowlby's work on attachment and loss, pioneered the idea that children need a secure base from which to widen their social circle.

However, cultural variations suggest that the way children show their attachment takes diverse forms. There is no one way in which children across the world show us that they are attached to the people they love. This is true for adults too. Some people like to go with a person they love to see them into the seat of the train, and to wave them goodbye. Others prefer to say their goodbyes at the ticket barrier and then to leave quickly, without looking back.

The importance of attachment and having a secure base are important issues in considering what helps, damages or constrains children as they develop their learning in a home setting, with a childminder or nanny, or in a group setting.

Manning-Morton and Thorp (2003), Elfer, Goldschmied and Selleck (2002) have researched this with reference to the key person approach which is used increasingly in day-care groups.

Being a key person for a child

It might seem beneficial to a child to have a key person who links with the child's family or carer. In practice, working with a group of practitioners, Manning-Morton and Thorp (2003) found these problems:

- The practitioners spend a great deal of time on domestic and household duties.
- Children are given factory-line care (everyone washed one after the other, or put to bed, etc.).
- Children are treated as a group rather than as individuals.
- Children tend to be ordered to do things, and regimented.
- Attachment is not seen as important.
- Practitioners are treated as a group, and seen as cogs of a machine, and therefore easy to replace.
- Parents are seen as separate from the nursery and not involved in it.

They point out that their findings, in a joint project between the London Borough of Camden and London Metropolitan University, resonate with the earlier work of Bain and Barnett (1980) and also complement those of Hopkins (1988). Although staff espoused in theory the young child's need for intimate and warm attachment to a key person, they did not develop these in practice, unless helped to do so through training which gave them strategies to do it within a job which made emotional demands on them.

Manning-Morton and Thorp therefore set up an accredited course of training, now widely used throughout the UK, which addresses the issues of working with very young children. Practitioners working in group day-care settings often feel either overwhelmed or frozen in their feelings. So practitioners need to be helped to recognize how they feel; understand what is happening; and develop strategies to deal with this for themselves, the parents and the children.

When a toddler cries bitterly as his/her mother leaves the nursery, the practitioner feels heartbroken and their natural reaction is to divert the child from how he/she feels. But the child needs to be allowed to feel. If the adult says, 'You don't like it when Mummy goes, do you? But she will be back later. Would you like to sit on my lap for a bit, because you are feeling sad?', the child often accepts this warm, sensitive support from the key worker, who is acknowledging how they feel.

Me and you

To be able to put yourself into another person's way of thinking and feeling is an incredible thing to be able to do. We see from the previous section that this is hard for adults.

Toddlers develop a sense of self, but since human beings are social animals, alongside this an understanding of others develops at the same time as walking, talking and pretending.

> *As soon as they can talk, children talk about their minds and those of other people. At first they concentrate on desires, perceptions and emotions: what they see, feel and want, rather than what they think or know. At around eighteen months, children start to develop pretend play. This requires an understanding of knowledge and belief – knowing what is real and what is not – and is one of the first instances of creativity. At around three, children start to talk about beliefs (e.g. 'I think the sweets are in the cupboard'). Only at the age of about four or five do children start to realise that people can have different beliefs from their own and that they themselves can have different beliefs at different times. This is referred to as having a 'Theory of Mind'.* (Blakemore, 2000: 6)

Predicting what someone else will do or feel

As with other aspects of developing learning, the theory of mind does not develop out of the blue. Children predict what someone else will do, feel and want before they can predict what someone thinks, knows or believes.

Even toddlers know that picking up their four-year-old brother's favourite toy car and walking off with it will provoke an angry reaction. The toddler is aware that although the car means nothing to him/her, it is an important object to his/her brother.

Predicting how someone else might feel

The same toddler might, later, when their brother has fallen over and is sobbing, looking at his grazed and stinging knee, go and fetch the toy car, and give it to him, knowing it will be a comfort. The car would not comfort the toddler after a fall, but he/she understands that different people have their feelings comforted in different ways.

Predicting someone's thoughts and beliefs

As Sarah-Jane Blakemore (2000) points out, children can understand what they experience through the senses. They might recognize that someone else likes different food from them. They might love bananas, but would not offer one to a friend because they know he/she does not like bananas. Understanding the different beliefs of people is a more difficult thing to be able to do. Frith (1992) has made an experiment which demonstrates the theory of mind. Children who can get inside someone else's head understand how it would be for Sally, returning to the room and looking for the marble (below).

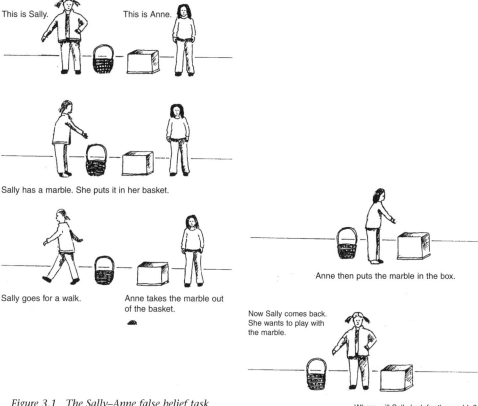

This is Sally.   This is Anne.

Sally has a marble. She puts it in her basket.

Sally goes for a walk.   Anne takes the marble out of the basket.

Anne then puts the marble in the box.

Now Sally comes back. She wants to play with the marble.

Figure 3.1   The Sally–Anne false belief task

Where will Sally look for the marble?

Observing children in natural settings rather than observing children in laboratory conditions

The Sally–Anne experiment is useful because it confirms the pioneering work of Judy Dunn, who began working in 1977 with Martin Richards on a longitudinal study in Cambridge and (later) in Pennsylvania. She says (1988: Preface), 'it seemed to me crucial to study children within their own families, rather than in an experimental setting'. She wanted to look at the impact of family experiences, and to find out not just what distresses or makes children feel insecure, but also what amuses, excites and interests them.

Her positive approach has led to a serious challenge to the traditional Freudian assertion that the birth of a sibling is linked to rivalry and disturbance. She found that there were no studies to test this. Her own, over many years, have revealed that things are more positive than Freudians have suggested. The issue is about the older sibling needing reassurance that he or she will be treated with equality alongside the new baby.

She began work with Carol Kendrick, an American psychologist, in 1982, and began to uncover some cracks in the traditional myths which have led us to a greater understanding of the theory of mind, linked with sibling relationships within, as she puts it, 'the drama and excitement of family life' (Dunn, 1988: Preface). She found that:

> Not only the firstborn children, but most surprisingly some of their younger siblings early in the second year showed a clear practical grasp of how to annoy or comfort other children. This suggested powers of understanding in these young children well beyond what we might expect from studies of children outside the familiar emotional world of the family. (Dunn, 1988: preface)

Revisiting Piaget

These two very different examples, from the work of Frith and Dunn, corroborate Piaget's major contribution to the field. Children are intellectually egocentric until the age of about four or five years, as Sarah-Jane Blakemore (2000) points out. They work their way towards understanding other people's ideas, thoughts and beliefs.

Dunn has shown us that from the time they walk, talk and pretend, they begin to understand other people's feelings, but only within the circle of people who love them and whom they love. This links with the experimental work of Margaret Donaldson (1978), which showed that children perform at a higher level when involved in tasks which make what she termed 'human sense' to them, and which are embedded in experiences which are familiar and meaningful to them.

Frith and Dunn's studies support Piaget's assertion (Piaget, 1947) that pseudo-concepts indicate the journey children take towards shedding intellectual egocentricity. However, this Piagetian term is rather a negative way of looking at children. It is more positive to use the more recent terminology, and instead of shedding egocentricity say that children develop theory of mind, first through the important relationships they have with people, which are bathed in emotion; then gradually move to understanding the beliefs and thoughts of others they do not know so intimately.

Different theories of mind

There are various different theories of mind. Ratey (2001: 140) suggests:

> *At one end is the opinion that the mind is the same as the brain, and at the other, that the mind is an entity completely separate from the brain, the result of a soul or some other attribute, and actually runs the machine called the brain. Somewhere in between these two oppositions is the idea that the mind is an emergent property of the brain – it is what results when the brain runs.*

The most important thing to remember is that each human being, for the rest of his or her life, will be constantly:

- creating understanding of the physical world and other people;
- reaffirming what is known;
- adding new understanding;
- at times changing their view of how things are;
- developing a world of symbolic layers.

The suggestion that the mind 'is what results when the brain runs', is helpful in teasing this out.

Developing theory of mind means that a child learns how to get inside the head and heart of someone else. The child can begin to understand the thoughts and feelings of another person. This is not the same as the emotional contagion seen in babies. They quickly 'catch' the feelings of other babies and people. When one baby starts to cry, others often start too.

Just as catching feelings is different from getting into the inside of someone else's head to understand how he/she thinks and feels, so empathy is not the same either. Empathy means recognizing how the other person feels because it is how you have felt on occasions.

Developing theory of mind goes further than this. Tom (three years) said to his mother, when his friend Jason came to play in his home, 'If he falls over, don't try to cuddle him. Just talk to him. He hates being cuddled like me.' Tom has empathy. He knows that his friend will need comforting if he hurts himself. He also has theory of mind because he has worked out that not everyone is comforted in the same way. Tom likes to be cuddled. Jason likes to be talked to.

The importance of memories

A powerful influence on the development of theory of mind is the development of episodic memories. The development of episodic memories helps young children to become conscious of their own thoughts and feelings and the feelings and thoughts of others. Carter (1998: 162) says:

Memories that remain clothed in personal detail are quite different, and the brain deals with them differently. These recollections, known as episodic memories, are usually cradled in a sense of time and space. They include the memory of 'being there' and are personal … When we recall them they recreate much of the state of mind we were in when they were laid down.

These kinds of memories (that recreate a previous state of mind) involve feelings as much as thought. Joseph Le Doux (in Carter, 1998: 98) stresses that 'the emotional part of our brain has more power to influence behaviour than the rational part'. This also resonates with Piaget's statement (which we shall explore later in the book) that you cannot have a thought without a feeling, but he also stresses that you cannot have a feeling without a thought.

Different kinds of memory

Procedural memory
How to ride a bike
Deeply ingrained habits
Stored in the cadate nucleus

Fear memory
Phobias

Flashbacks
Stored in the amygdala

Episodic memory
Personal and emotional
Representing past experience
Stored in different bits of the cortex
Retrieved through the frontal cortex

Semantic memory
Facts registered by cortex
Encoded in cortical regions in temporal lobe
Retrieval through frontal lobes

Feelings, the foundations of memories

Holding on to our experiences helps us to learn. We can use the past and build practical working theories about how we and other people are likely to behave, feel and think. This capability probably developed from physical evolutionary survival systems.

According to Carter (2002: 158), feelings bind our sensory perceptions, feelings and memories in a seamless whole. Knowing that feelings are fundamental to thinking helps us to care about the nurturing we give to young children, which is embedded in the time we spend with them. The development of consciousness and theory of mind go hand in hand in developing learning.

However, we can also see that understanding how someone else thinks, and what their belief systems are helps us to communicate, share and exchange thoughts, and to develop abstract and higher-order thoughts as part of a human group.

In practice

- Do you have a key person system in place?
- Do you talk in soft voices to children, looking at them while you do so, so that they feel valued?
- Do you talk with your colleagues about how you feel when you have spent time with a child who has been challenging or distressed? Is this a valued and important part of the way your team works together?
- Do you focus on finding what helps children to be at their most calm and open to learning, when they are challenging, have special educational needs and disabilities or are easily ignored? Are you on their side? Or are you trying to control and shape them so that they give you an easier life?
- Do you create an atmosphere in which children who are challenging are not rejected by other children, which will happen if you show constant disapproval and make judgements about them?

Further reading

Davies, M. (2003) *Movement and Dance in Early Childhood*, 3rd edn. London: Paul Chapman Publishing.

Forbes, R. (forthcoming) *Beginning to Play from Birth to Three*. Maidenhead: Open University Press.

Manning-Morton J. and Thorp, M. (2003) *Key Times for Play: The First Three Years*. Maidenhead: Open University Press.

Nielsen, L. (1992) *Space and Self: Active Learning by Means of the Little Room*. Sikon (available from RNIB).

Orr, R. (2003) *My Right to Play: A Child with Complex Needs*. Maidenhead: Open University Press.

4

Social and cultural development

Key themes

In this chapter we highlight a few examples of the many socio-cultural influences on children developing learning. These are:

- knives when learning about food preparation;
- books as powerful cultural artefacts through which children participate in their community;
- dance, which is arguably the most ancient form of cultural experience.

We explore the way that adults teach the culture, through both direct and indirect means. We look at some of the issues leading to converging views, which result in solidarity of thought between those with either a biological or a socio-cultural emphasis when working with children as they develop their learning.

At the Castlebrae Family Centre. Nicole sees people using knives to prepare and eat food. Jeannie, Nicole's mother, joins in with the group of parents cutting fruit. Nicole does a great deal of watching what is going on, twiddling a bowl as she does so. Her mother helps her to use the knife. She then has a go by herself. She smiles as she is given the freedom and responsibility of doing this on her own.

The knife is more than an object for cutting. It is part of the culture in which Nicole is growing up. She already wants to use one because she has worked out that it is high status to use a knife. It is an adult thing to do, and she strives to act like an adult, as part of participating in the culture. She knows what a knife is for. Not all cultures or families use knives. Some use chop-sticks, or fingers. The important thing here is that Nicole's sense of who she is and how she relates to others is influenced by objects which are cultural artefacts.

Children are very attracted to the cultural artefacts they see adults using. They seem to recognize early on that these are significant objects for the adults who are important to them. When children see adults with books and preparing food, the objects they are using become prime cultural artefacts for them and highly desirable. Using such objects as adults do is attractive for young children, as they strive to take part in their culture.

Because the lives of young children are utterly dependent on the adults who care for them and work with them, they are inevitably eager to join in with what adults do, and to use the cultural artefacts they think are important.

A knife is a socio-cultural tool

Books creating access to the culture

As a newborn baby Nicole and her mother Jeannie were part of the Craigmillar Books for Babies project. Books are an example of artefacts which are a central part of the culture that Nicole is participating in. Because adults introduced her to books from babyhood, she knew they existed from an early age. In many cultures books are important for inclusion in society. Those who cannot read or write find it difficult to participate fully in the culture. It is no wonder that parents give these cultural activities great priority. Davies (2003: 2) points out that parents put a great deal of energy, time and effort into encouraging reading and writing. It is sad when other aspects of cultural life are neglected, such as the visual arts, drama, dance and music, or the ability to be a creative, problem-solving scientist (Bruce, 2001a).

The Books for Babies project workers show how this careful introduction works for both the babies and their parents and carers.

Newborn
The family will be invited to join Craigmillar Books for Babies and given a board book by the health visitor.

Two months
A Baby Book Bag containing another book and items including a book list, information, a poster, rhyme cards, a height chart and library membership forms will be given at the health clinic visit. The project worker will be there to talk with the parent or carer about sharing books with babies.

Seven months
A Bookstart Bag containing two books and items including information, a nursery rhyme place mat and a book list will be given at the health clinic visit. The project worker will be there to talk with the parent or carer about sharing books with babies.

Ten months to one year
The project worker will visit the family in its own home and offer a further chance to claim another book from the local library to share with the baby.

Two years
Another free book is chosen from a selection of books at the child's two-year-old check.

Three years
A Transition to Nursery Event, for children turning three. 'This is an opportunity for parents to chat informally with service providers about any concerns or questions they may have as their child begins nursery … . As always there will be songs, rhymes and activities.' Each child is given a rucksack and a book. Individual invitations are sent out to all families on the database with children turning three.

Throughout the first three years

Events and outreach work

The project continues to offer families support through a variety of contacts such as home visits, drop-in groups and library events, with a variety of ways for parents and children to explore language and develop important family habits that foster good communication and learning together. Through these events and other more informal contact the project provides a number of resources such as leaflets, posters and other literacy-related materials.

At the end of each month there is a Rhyme Time Event. In February 2002 it was 'Dancing snowflakes' led by Lyn Tarlton.

Newsletter

All these events are described in a quarterly newsletter with details of Craigmillar Books for Babies events and other information, including rhymes and books. Enjoyable ways to develop early language are also recommended.

There is also information about other resources in the area, such as parent and toddler groups, nursery education and adult learning. Parents or carers will be referred to other agencies and services for advice and guidance.

Bringing up children in a fast-changing world is hard for parents and carers (Kalliala, 2004, in press). Not all parents enjoyed reading books during their own childhood, and many have bad memories of the experience at school with formal, narrow teaching methods. It is very helpful to all parents to have support in areas which the culture emphasizes as important, such as literacy. People in the UK who are not confident readers and writers are in difficulties. Here are some of the things the parents who were part of the Craigmillar project said.

Katie's mum
It was good to get the books so early. Katie has got to like them more because of this. The books were there so we didn't have to wait until we got around to buying them. As we had the books there in the house, we used them.

Katie has joined the library and takes books out. We go to Books for Babies events and Katie can even say the word 'library'.

Dale's mum
Books for Babies is a good idea. It helps kids. Dale still has the books and we've bought him some more.

We come along to the events at the library. Every time we go to the library, Dale says: 'Books for Babies!' I like it when other people come along to do the rhyme times. The storyteller was very good. I liked the puppet workshop – it was a laugh!

It's an extra wee thing to do, a nice wee change. Dale goes straight for the toys whenever he goes to the library. It's nice for Dale to meet other children and it lets me relax a bit more and sit about.

Books for Babies helps Dale along. He is learning through looking at the books and the pictures. Now he can see things and say them. It's helped me to teach him more.

Giving out books at the clinic is a good idea because some people may not go along to Books for Babies events at the library. I think books should be given to kids.

The co-ordinator's report

Projects such as this one are having an important effect. The co-ordinator's report shows what an exciting journey has taken place. It is an inspiration to other practitioners while giving very practical ways forward.

Craigmillar has a long history of community activism and development; however, this work is set against a backdrop of stark need … .

When the project was first proposed in 1996, 40% of the first years at the local High School had a reading age of nine or less. Nursery school teachers in the area had significant numbers of children attending with speech difficulties, which meant that by the time these children reached primary school age they could be up to two years behind in terms of development.

Local library membership of under fours was poor, despite an extensive outreach programme and promotion of the library to parents and carers. There were only 5% active registered members in this age range. This suggested that parents were not bringing younger children into the library and it was only when the child went to nursery or school that they were exposed to books and reading.

Reading the co-ordinator's report and seeing what the parents said and how the families are actively involved in introducing books to their young children is heartening. It is also in line with government policies of the day.

Walking, talking and pretending

We have seen that walking, talking and pretending develop together during the toddler period.

Books are another kind of socio-cultural tool

Walking as a cultural event

Adults who encourage their babies to walk often put furniture at carefully placed distances. Then babies can make a dash for it from one piece to another. Thus they literally stay on their feet, as they make the transition from babyhood to toddler times. The adults and older children will cheer and encourage the tottering walker to keep going, and delight in the success of walking. When adults and older children help development along, they cause learning to happen.

Talking as a cultural event

It is difficult to stop children learning to talk, unless they are deprived of human company, do not hear people talking or are not spoken to.

Adults can be very helpful to children as they learn language. When talking to babies and toddlers, as Trevarthen points out (1998), it is very difficult not to speak in a high pitch and with rhythm, speaking slowly. We are naturally inclined to do this. But, as Elizabeth Bates (1999, Programme 1) emphasizes, adults are most helpful when they also stress the important words and point at the things they are talking about. The intellectual life of the young child is bound up in understanding how things happen in space and time, and the reasons for events and situations.

Using symbols of the culture

Children cannot know what dancing is unless someone shows them dances and encourages them to join in. Or is that entirely true? It does seem that we are inclined to imitate others. However, this is not the same as copying. Imitation involves taking an idea and re-jigging it to suit another context. Nicole might have seen someone using knives to carve meat, or slice bread, but she is able to take the idea of cutting with a knife, and to cut a banana and other fruits. The brain is naturally inclined towards some kinds of activity, such as imitation and being part of what other people do, especially the people significant in the child's life. We are also biologically driven to walk, talk and imagine, and imitate. It is in our brain to develop these aspects of being human.

We have seen that parents are encouraged by the culture of the UK to place great priority on cultural artefacts which are linked with learning to read and write. But the broader, richer and deeper the cultural artefacts and experiences children take part in as active, involved participants, the more likely they are to become bookworms and enthusiastic lifelong learners.

The Books for Babies project will be most successful if it operates alongside other cultural events, such as dancing, music and drama, which give children a sense of self, interdependent with those they love and are loved by.

Participating in dances and music

At the Children's House Nursery School, the children (between three and five years old) are introduced to the dances of their culture. These include traditional Scottish dancing, dances from Ghana and contemporary disco dances. Many of the parents were brought up on Scottish dances, and readily join in with the staff to encourage the children to participate. The caretaker and a nursery nurse teach the children the dance. One mother grew up in Ghana. The nursery valued this connection and invited Gift Amu Logotse, an African storyteller, to come to the school with his stories, drums and dances.

Cross-cultural patterns in dance

In Wales and Northern Ireland learning the heritage of cultural artefacts and symbols is also part of the curriculum. In Wales children also learn Welsh. The English document, 'Curriculum Guidance for the Foundation Stage' (DFES/QCA, 2000), does not emphasize a clearly identifiable English cultural heritage.

Dances and music from Ghana

Scottish and African dances have particular steps and country dances of all cultures are as old as humanity, as Paul Harris (2000: ix) points out:

> *In the Upper Paleolithic, a period that began approximately 40,000 years ago, a revolution in human culture occurred. This revolution is frequently attributed either to the onset, or the sudden acceleration, of a new and distinctive human genitive capacity. One line of interpretation has emphasised a change in the depth of temporal organisation. Tools were increasingly produced well in advance of their actual use; dwelling sites were created with a lengthy period of occupation in mind. However, alongside this shift in the organisation of food and shelter, another set of activities emerged that can be less easily linked to the pragmatics of survival: cave painting, the diversification and stylisation of tools, the manufacture of bodily ornaments and new burial practices.*

Children who have danced in any country dances gain from the experience. They contain circular patterns, linear patterns, skipping, jumping and running. In Scottish and Ghanaian dances all of these are found, but in different forms. They are also found in the dances of ancient cultures across the world. From a repertoire of movements, common to everyone, variations emerge, which signal the essence of each culture's dances. The steps may be linked with schemas, that is, patterns of behaviour common to the brain's development in all cultures (Athey, 1990).

Let us look at some of the children at Children's House Nursery School and how they joined in the dances.

Scottish dances

It is part of the Scottish curriculum framework to learn about the Scottish heritage: dances, steps and literature.

Some children listen to the music of a local Scottish piper (the janitor) while others dance to the music. There is no pressure to perform the correct steps. In fact, as Baker (2002) points out, 'Claire and Jodie enjoyed more than thirty minutes making up their own dances and taking turns being the leader.' They dressed up in tartan skirts and bands over their clothes.

Their dancing was heavily influenced by their knowledge of Scottish dancing. They dosi-doed, skipped about and moved their arms in the traditional forms of the folk dances. They invited an adult to join in. Claire is a very confident Scottish dancer, and other children follow her as she skips along, with her hands on her hips. She and Jodie have 'the look' that is both full of involvement in the dance and focused along with the look of sheer joy that accompanies the major achievement of co-ordinating dance steps to the satisfaction of the dancers together.

There is nothing like participating in a group that makes music or dances. It brings feelings of the deepest satisfaction, and also of being part of a collective self, which gives a sense of belonging. A sense of belonging is central to the principles of diversity (Bruce and Meggitt, 2002: 1–2).

Children and families need to feel part of things. It is especially important if they belong to a minority group that they feel both valued, respected and included. Children need to build positive images of themselves, supported by those around them. When they are narrowly stereotyped they cannot develop as fully as they should. Because most discriminatory behaviour is unintended, it is important to help practitioner families become aware of what it means, and to think of ways to avoid behaving in ways which discriminate against other people.

Circle dances

Interestingly, circle dances, which are cross-cultural, have been used historically to control dancers. It is difficult to go wild as you dance when holding hands in a circle. There is a place for circle dances and games, but these should not dominate. They are a good way of making groups of dancers feel safe and secure. 'Ring games are a favourite all year round – there is plenty of space in the garden and the children often organise themselves and play ring games together.' (Baker, 2002)

Creating space for dance indoors and outdoors

At Children's House there is an area with enough space to dance in. Sometimes the children make their own music with drums and other instruments put out for them. At other times they choose music available. This will vary according to the current curriculum. At present there is an interest in ballet.

Tuning into the movements of those you dance with

> Tom and Liam enjoy making up their own dance routine. They select shimmering trousers to wear over their clothes. As happens when people dance together in formations, they have half an eye out for the movement of their dance partner, so that they concentrate on making little steps with their feet in synchrony. They dance side by side, and every so often Liam turns to Tom and smiles. The dance resonates with the small balletic steps they have seen.
>
> As the music revs up in the way that ballet music does when it starts a frenzied crescendo, Tom and Liam really use the clothes. They have put on the bodiced petticoats and they begin: 'swirling and birling with the fine materials of the skirts watching each other respond to the tempo of the music, making up their own cameos. Drama was introduced as they interpret the music. Posters and books of ballet dancers were also readily available.' (Baker, 2001)
>
> Chelsie and Brandon are letting the music lead them. Chelsie is wearing a similar outfit as Sophie's. Brandon has donned glittering trousers over his clothes, like Tom and Liam. They are watching other children to give them ideas, and then they allow the music to take them. They are responding to others and responding to music, rather than choreographing steps which they can repeat at will and perform.
>
> Tom and Liam started by making their own dance steps, in a choreographed sense that they could repeat the sequences. Once the music began to dominate, as it became more and more inviting, they moved into responding to music rather than choreographing. Children need to experience both, but it is helpful if adults working with them bear in mind which is which. There is a tendency to encourage responding to music rather than choreography in the early years (Davies, 2003).

Tom and Liam enjoy making up their own dance routine, while Sophie is quite happily absorbed in her own dance

Working on choreographing a solo

In the same dance space, Sophie works on a solo. She is completely absorbed in choreographing her dance. She is wearing a calf-length frilly petticoat with a plain nylon bodice. She focuses on both her feet and arms. Her feet make little running steps on demi-points. Her arms are held straight out in front and her head is held high. Her dance, like the dance choreographed by Tom and Liam, ripples with ballet-like steps. The children are not being influenced by each other. They have their own dance agenda to carry through to their satisfaction, resulting in a quite separate partner dance and a solo.

Professional choreographers usually choose the music they use after they have made the dance, and this is useful to bear in mind when working with choreography with children.

Maureen Baker (2002) writes, 'Four boys made up their own dance. Here the music came second. The important thing was the making of the dance together.' Co-ordinating four dancers together is a very sophisticated thing to manage to do. This dance could have been repeated later on another occasion. It is the beginning of performance.

Performance

Children are aware from an early age that some sorts of dancing require an audience, such as ballet. The children made a stage out of large 'Community Playthings' hollow blocks. They do not make a stage when they begin Scottish dancing. They are beginning to distinguish between folk, community dances and more elite, specialist dances.

They show by this that they already know a huge amount about the culture they are growing up in.

Dances from Ghana

In Children's House Nursery School there is a family from Ghana. Because the local families are not so knowledgeable about dance from this part of Africa, Fran, a parent, helps the school to introduce this into the curriculum. Together with Gift Amu Logoste, who plays the drums, she dresses in traditional costume and dances for the children at group time. Several children join in. Interestingly, Bradley, a confident disco dancer, leads this, and draws Marcus in to dance with him. The two boys wear the Ghanaian costumes on offer, and dance in the traditional way of men as dance partners together, influenced by the way they have seen Fran dance.

From disco dancing to Ghanaian dances

Bradley demonstrates powerfully what Gopnik et al. (1999) stress in their ground-breaking book. We use what we know to help us do what we do not know how to do, and we need other people to help us. Bradley uses his knowledge of disco dancing to access the traditional dance forms of Ghana.

He also uses his knowledge of Western music rhythms to access African drum rhythms. Conversely, Amy, Fran's daughter, uses what she knows of Ghanaian dances to enable her to try out disco dancing, on another occasion. She and Gary dance together in partnership in the home corner. She puts her left arm on his shoulder, and then holds Gary's hand with her other arm. They look thrilled with themselves as they perform this feat to the music.

Ballroom dances – co-ordinating the steps

Clare and Bradley enjoy modelling the man and woman holds as they dance in the home corner in a waltz-inspired manner. Bradley puts his right arm round Claire's shoulder, and holds her hand with his left hand. Claire puts her left arm round his waist and holds his hand with her right arm. Nearly there! They do not look so thrilled with themselves. They sense that this is not quite right.

When to teach directly and indirectly

It is always a question for adults to know when to teach directly and when to leave children to work things out for themselves. This is where practitioners who know their children and how much experience they have of dance use their professional judgement. Only those who have this can act intuitively, because intuition is based on an edifice of knowledge.

It also depends on adults knowing enough about different dance forms themselves. Sometimes children know more than we do (Bruce, 2001).

Bradley is able to perform quite intricate disco steps which he has learnt from his family and at the dance classes he has attended. He can lead his partner Shannon, so that although she does not know as much as he does, she can simply allow herself to be moved by him, in the traditional way a man leads the woman dancer in ballroom dancing and some disco dances.

He stands facing her and they hold hands. He then raises his arms, crossing them over as he goes, and turning his partner with his arms crossed in the air. Again the two children look thrilled as the steps come right.

There is an exhilaration in their expressions. Moments of learning like this are to be treasured. He is applying the knowledge he has about disco dancing, but with a partner he has not danced with before, which makes it a new experience.

Bradley, the disco dancer, adds some more elaborate moves to his dance with his partner

We learn to dance by dancing

Bradley demonstrated some of the moves he had learnt at the disco dancing classes he attended out of school on other occasions. For instance, one involved lying on his stomach, raising his body on his arms and spreading his legs apart. He is not usually interested in demonstrating steps to others, and usually dances without teaching others. When he danced with Shannon, he initiated her into the dance by leading her as they danced. We learn to dance by dancing. But we also learn to dance by applying what we have seen others do in their dances.

The children at Children's House Nursery School know about Scottish dancing because they are growing up in Scotland. Some know about disco dancing as part of the culture of the UK and the world beyond. They have also been introduced to dances and music from Ghana by the staff of the school working closely with expertise in the community (Fran, a parent) and inviting outside expertise to join in (Gift Amu Logotse).

The socio-cultural aspects of developing learning

We learn our culture, and the canon of knowledge society values, through dances, paintings, drawings, sculptures, architecture, nature study, sciences and mathematical insights, with stories, poetry, and reading and writing, all of which open up the world of higher thinking for us.

The influences of other people on children, together with the events, places and the cultural context in which children grow up are of prime importance to their development. We can call these the socio-cultural aspects of developing learning. The social relationships children engage in may cultivate development, or constrain and damage it.

The cultural experiences we have will bring about particular ways of viewing the world. Some children experience and actively take part in several cultures. Others grow up in mono-cultural worlds. Children who grow up in a mono-cultural situation are seriously disadvantaged, lacking the flexibility and understanding of other ways of doing things or thinking which psychologists call the theory of mind explored in this book.

Nurture and nature

The socio-cultural and biological aspects of development, which are interdependent, are paramount for young children developing their learning. Researchers have favoured one or the other in what is historically known as the nature–nurture debate, in which the socio-cultural is nurture, and the biological, genetic, brain development is nature.

Unfortunately, this has often polarized people to support one or the other. But in fact nature depends on nurture and nurture cannot exist unless there is nature to nurture.

No one grand narrative about how children develop their learning

Lyotard (1979) a postmodern theorist, called for the end of what he called the 'grand narrative' approach to looking at developing learning. He argued that we cannot take one theory or perspective on how children develop and learn.

While there are different ways of looking at how children develop and learn, this does not mean that all perspectives are as good as each other. If we are too eclectic, we shall find ourselves using approaches which contradict each other. That leads to thoroughly confused practice, with no inner logic to our view of children.

We need to be consistent in our work with children. The best way forward is to find converging evidence, which forms areas of solidarity between different theories when developing learning in young children.

Evolutionary approaches

Dahlberg et al. (1999: 17) aim to create: 'a crisis in people's thinking which will open up new possibilities and expectations, alternative enquiries and solutions, opportunities for new understandings and new ways of seeing, visions of accessible futures which neither reflect a nostalgic longing for the past nor assume a pessimistic outlook.'

This suggests that practitioners need to be in a constant state of revolution in order to keep their thinking and practice alive.

This is quite different from Gammage's proposal (in David et al., 2002) that we need to keep re-analysing the theories we know, love and use. This is an evolutionary approach to keeping practice alive and moving forward. In this book the second approach is taken.

We need to remember that as well as having a limited cultural context, any theory about developing learning in children will also have a limited range.

- Some theories help us to look at the developing brain throughout evolution.
- Some theories help us to look at current knowledge of the way a human brain develops.
- Some help us to look at the child's developing learning about cultural aspects.
- Some give help with understanding children's feelings and relationships.

We need to know which theories are good for what. Gopnik et al. (1999: 157) suggest that humans: 'never start from scratch; instead they modify and change what they already know to gain new knowledge. But they are never permanently dogmatic – the things they know (or think they know) are always open to further revision.'

We often change our thinking about practice when we come across some-thing that is nearly like what we do. In some early childhood settings there may be a group story-time first thing in the morning. In others a group story may be told at the end of the session. This is what Carter (2002: 202) calls a 'near-to' situation, and it makes us think and challenges what we do. Practi-tioners in each setting will reflect on which might be best for their group of children and families.

Using what we know to develop our practice

We can look at the work of pioneers of early childhood practice, such as Friedrich Froebel in the nineteenth century or Margaret McMillan in devel-oping nursery schools in the early 1900s. It is helpful to juxtapose what they did with what postmodernists such as Burman (1994) and Dahlberg et al. (1999) argue.

- We can see if we can find any common ground between the thinking of the early pioneers and these thinkers of today.
- This will help us to look at our terminology and update it in ways which build on the past. We can use what we know to learn more, and adjust our 'near-to' concepts.
- We can see if there are subtle or stark differences in thinking between the pioneers and the post-modern thinkers. Are there any 'near-to' practices?
- This will help us to see what we want to continue doing, and what we need to adapt, change or discard.
- Unless we look at what has gone before, we are likely to discard too much. Using what we know about the past and present in these ways helps us into the future. The exercise is invaluable.

When we study current theories, and see where they agree and disagree, it helps us to think about which ones we find give us some guidance in our practice. It becomes fascinating to find out when they are so much in dis-agreement that using one means you cannot use the other, because that would lead to contradictions.

It is very helpful when theories have areas of agreement which give insight to practitioners in ways which reveal that there is converging evidence, giving areas of solidarity between the theories. Then practitioners feel strong about using several theories at once. This is the way theory is used in this book.

In practice

- Is your setting at the heart of your community? Do you actively involve parents by encouraging them to participate?
- When a child and family join your community, are there things and ways of doing things in place which make them feel they belong?
- How do you value the culture of each child?
- Do you introduce children to the food, clothes, artefacts, dances, music, art, languages and social etiquettes of all who are part of this community?
- Do you introduce a carefully chosen range of literature and non-fiction books to help children and families reflect and learn about other people in the community and beyond?
- Do you see each child as an individual, with a unique personality and particular interests? What do you do to make sure there is something for that child in your setting every day he or she attends?

Further reading

Brookson, M. and Spratt, J. (2001) 'When We Have Choices, We Can Have Vision: An Exploration of Play Based on an Observation in Reggio Emilia', *Early Childhood Practice: The Journal for Multi-Professional Partnerships* 3(2): 11–24.

David, T., Gooch, K., Powell, S. and Abbott, L. (2002) 'Review of the Literature to Support Birth to Three Matters: A Framework to Support Children in their Earliest Years'. DFES/Sure Start.

Davies, M. (2003) *Movement and Dance in Early Childhood*, 2nd edn. London: Paul Chapman Publishing.

Murray, L. and Andrews, L. (2000) *The Social Baby: Understanding Babies' Communication from Birth*. Richmond, Surrey: CP Publishing.

Woodhead, M., Faulkner, D. and Littleton, K. (1998) *Cultural Worlds of Early Childhood*. London: Routledge/Open University Press.

5

Communication

Key themes

Communication is a very important human process, and babies engage in communicating with others from the start of their lives. We communicate with ourselves and with other people. We use words or signs to do this, but we also communicate with our body language and gestures, our facial expressions, the sounds and movements we make, and the way we pause and are silent.

We use symbols in our dances, music, visual arts, in the poetry we write and in the stories we tell, act out in drama or write down as literature. Much of this book is about different aspects of communication.

Human beings are the only animals who communicate in such symbolic ways. We are sociable animals, living for the most part in communities and families. Talking about events (past, present and future), ideas, feelings and relationships is therefore of great importance. The human brain has an enormous propensity for communication through sophisticated symbol use. It is important that we do not provide the kinds of experiences which cause children to be left only able to use symbols in narrow and purely functional ways, because this wastes the possibilities for thinking, feeling and relating to others.

One of the greatest pleasures of working with young children is to see their fascination with and eagerness for communication of many kinds. We owe it to them not to destroy or damage this faculty, and to cultivate it with respect and sensitivity.

Interaction with self and others

Communication is first about getting in contact with ourselves, so that we are, as the saying goes, in touch with ourselves. Second, communication is about getting in touch with and exchanging meaning with others. Sometimes we use words to do this, sometimes we do not. To do so we use movement, music, sounds, and visual, tactile, olfactory and taste experiences as well as images and representations.

Sometimes we talk silently to ourselves. When we do this, according to Bendall (2003: 1), we use our phonological loop. This helps us to learn new words.

At times we may talk out loud to ourselves. This also helps us to become more conscious of what we are saying to ourselves. Adults may not admit to this, but in fact both children and adults frequently talk to themselves.

The phonological loop co-ordinates with what Bendall calls our 'visuo-spatial sketchpad', and helps us to make on-the-spot decisions. We are influenced by the way what we see connects with what we hear.

Most of us spend most of our time with other people. There are huge cultural variations in the amount of time people spend communicating.

In reality, most of us live in several different communities. An early childhood setting is one kind of community that a child and family might become part of. The family is another. Most of the communicating that takes place in the home is natural learning. The interactions and communications between people in home situations are informal.

Herding children into large groups

In an earlier book (Bruce, 1997: 142) I wrote of the problems of herding children into groups for parts of their day. This discourages sensitive communication, damages the social and moral development and the feelings of children, and constrains their thoughts and ideas.

When a child is constantly part of a large group of children, the 'bystander effect' (Kitzinger, 1997: 16) happens. It means that a child is less likely to respond to a situation in a thoughtful way, and is more likely to stay as a passive member of a crowd, conforming to what the other children do. Children in smaller, intimate, high-quality settings are more likely to develop a sensitive, caring and thoughtful approach with skilful communication and language.

Britton (1987) hopes that, just as family life encourages natural communication, so we will also avoid using early childhood settings or schools as opportunities to introduce formal teaching, stilted communication and unnatural communication.

When these things happen, practitioners do not communicate with children with sincerity and genuine discussions. They talk at children, making remarks which are not authentic, such as 'We don't do that, do we?' This inevitably distances the staff from the children. This can easily occur when children are taught as one large group. 'It is clear that we have a choice: we can operate so as to make as rich an interactive learning community as we can, or we may continue to treat it [the school or early years setting] as a captive audience for whatever instruction we choose to offer.' (Britton, 1987: 26)

Developing communication, language and literacy

In earlier chapters we have seen how the development of Christopher, Nicole and other children growing up in the Castlebrae community is an interactive communication process. Interaction with others (Bruce, 1987) is central to the development of communication and language, and later literacy development. An interactionist approach offers practical and theoretically consistent and helpful insights for practitioners working to find effective ways of communicating with children and their families.

Sharing an experience

When there is good communication and interaction between parents, practitioners and children in a setting, learning develops with quality. Staff and parents took some children from Children's House to the local hospital. This visit did not just arise out of nowhere. Like every other aspect of creating a learning environment, visits should be for a reason. The reason for this visit was that Sarah, who attends Children's House nursery school, was in hospital. It is significant that after the visit, Amy decided to write to Sarah. This visit would help children to understand more about hospitals.

Emma, who also attends the school, has weekly physiotherapy in the school, and goes to the hospital to have her 'stookies' (plaster casts) fitted. Again, the visit increases the children's understanding of what is involved in going to hospital. Other children have seen relatives, involved in fights, heart attacks, strokes and falls, who have needed urgent treatment. The visit helps them to understand more about how hospitals treat patients. The visit also helps adults and children to increase their vocabularies as they learn together.

'I am writing a card to Sarah because she was in the hospital'

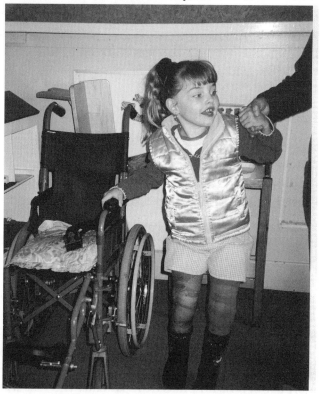

Emma with stookies on both her legs

Communicating by looking at photographs

When Gary saw himself and his mother in a photograph after the visit, he said to the nursery nurse looking at the photographs with him, 'My Mummy was taking the stethoscope.' As he looked at the next photo he said, 'I am hearing my Mummy's chest.' On the visit the staff talked with (not at) the children and parents about what they experienced together. They saw a row of crutches hanging in a store-room. When looking at the book of photographs the staff put next to the hospital play area to follow up the visit, Jodie said, 'The crutches – for sore legs – Jade my big cousin fell off Brandon's bike and she needed crutches.' Aaron said, 'There are all walking sticks – my auntie Violet has a walking stick so that she doesn't fall – not in the house, just outside.'

Communicating by making play scenarios

In the hospital play area, Aaron pretends to be the patient, with the support of the teacher, who pretends to be the nurse, while Claire listens to her chest with the stethoscope. Claire then pretends to be the patient and puts on the stookie. On another day, she lies down in the hospital play area and pretends to be the patient, saying, 'I hurt my heart – Aaron gave me the mask to help me.'

The hospital play is also offered outdoors. Here the children set up their own hospital and enjoy the play in another context.

Gary (four years old) playing at making X-rays using the photocopier, said: 'I'll put ma hand in there and the picture will come out of the bottom – there. Make it work – press the button – the wee light is like that – that looks like green it makes something different – another light there see. Do the hand again! Yours hand mine hand.' (Baker, 2001)

Gary continued his interest in the skeleton (from the X-rays) and borrowed a nursery video to watch at home. He often drew skeletons and went to the classroom poster, pointing to bones and running his fingers over it. His friend Bradley said: 'Gary must like skeletons. I have got a skeleton and I have got skin and veins. Veins carry blood all through your body – if blood stops you die. Guns can kill, injure you and you never come alive – two of my people have died.' (Baker, 2001)

Parents supporting play scenarios

One of the parents, supporting children in their small-world hospital play, said: 'Hospital play helps the children if their mum is in hospital having a baby. It gives them more knowledge that hospital isn't all doom and gloom and helps them understand that there is more to the ambulance going round with its flashing light. The posters, books and figures in the nursery made it easier for me to help explain things because I had the book and Ali was able to play with the wee figures.' (Baker, 2001)

Amy, who wrote to Sarah in hospital, enjoys the feeling of control as she makes her own hospital stories with the small world. In this way, she deals with her fears and manages them. Play helps children to communicate with themselves. This is particularly important where feelings are concerned.

Non-verbal communication

Non-verbal communication forms 85 percent of all communication with others, but it differs according to the cultural context. For example, greetings vary in different parts of the world. They are also often spoken and use particular movements, like kissing, shaking hands, bowing or nodding the head.

Talking with others cannot take place in isolation from non-verbal communication. If you try to say something without moving, it is very difficult, if not impossible to do so without facial expression, eye contact, body language and hand gestures (Acredelo and Goodwyn,1997), intonation, rhythm and phrasing, turn-taking, pauses, awareness of the listener in a conversation (such as bending the head to listen) or sharing a focus together. We listen to what others say to us using what we know of the sounds of our mother tongue or other familiar languages.

The teacher at Greengables is doing something which staff in early years settings do all the time. Sue is helping a three-year-old girl to hang up her painting to dry. However, the way that she does this is crucial. She communicates non-verbally in ways which encourage Susan 'to have a go'. She bends down to be near her so that they can easily have eye contact. She also talks with her, suggesting how to hang the painting, and remarking that she particularly likes the way she has made arched lines in stripes of different colours. Then she pauses, and waits, which allows her the time to reply. Susan tells her that it is a rainbow.

Sue has, through the discussion, taught her how to hang up her painting, and showed she values the painting. They have exchanged information, as happens in a good conversation.

There can be communication without words, but it is almost impossible to communicate in words without some kind of non-verbal communication, which language experts now believe to be at least 85 percent of all communication.

Most non-verbal communication is through our bodies. Our bodies communicate how we think, feel, and relate to others. We give each other signals without words, although most of the time, we are not aware that we are doing this.

Communication beyond ourselves – the universe

We can also communicate non-verbally through the arts, as we dance or make music together, and through two-dimensional drawings and paintings and three-dimensional models and sculptures. We tend to think of non-verbal communication in relation to our body language. It is also bound up in the way we communicate without words through the arts. Weaving, painting, drawing, sculpture, dances, music are all part of the non-verbal ways in which we speak to each other. At Children's House a clothes-horse has been turned into a weaving frame by the entrance. Anyone who fancies – parents, staff and children – can add something to it with bits of wool, ribbon, raffia, straw, twigs threaded through. People express themselves in this way, and it is often possible to say who did what, because people communicate their personalities through this kind of non-verbal communication. In all my years of working in early childhood services, I have never seen this emphasized. I make two categories of non-verbal communication:

- through our bodies and facial expressions and voices
- through the art forms which do not use words, such as dance, music and the visual arts.

Below we shall see the importance of understanding evolution and the early history of *homo sapiens* (the human being).

Spoken or signed communication

Communication can also reach deep levels of thinking and feeling when spoken or signed language is used. The development of communication involves different kinds of interaction. We communicate with ourselves as we think, as well as communicating with other people. Our brains and genetic make-up play a part, and so do the people we meet and the experiences we have.

A group of connectionist researchers (Elman et al., 1996) who stress the importance of what they describe as 'Interactions all the way down' argue that 'The developmental process is one of the most amazing mysteries in the universe' (p. 319) because 'Nature has solved the problem of building complex bodies with minimal information' (p. 320).

Co-ordination and the brain

Some animals are born almost fully developed, but human children are born rather undeveloped compared with, say, a bird or a snail. Childhood in human children is a crucial time in developing learning because this is the time when those aspects of brain development which are innate interact with people and the physical world.

Elman et al. argue that our 'genes are the conductor who orchestrates these interactions' (p. 321). Different parts of the brain interact with each other, such as gesture and movement, sound identification and production, vision, etc. In this chapter we are concerned with the interactions involving communication. Like every other aspect of development, communication is part of the many networks and webs woven throughout development, and continually changed by learning. 'If developmental paths were always straight and always uphill, they would not be nearly as interesting as they are.' (Elman et al., 1996: 42)

Cognitive psychologists and interactions within the brain

It is not only the group of researchers called connectionists who emphasize the interactions and co-ordinations between different parts of the brain. Gopnik et al. (1999: 127) who are cognitive psychologists, suggest that the sense, movement and communication systems interact with each other.

Early prehistorians and interactions within the brain

From a very different perspective, Steven Mithen, professor of early prehistory at the University of Reading, suggests that the main difference between Neanderthal people and *homo sapiens* lies in the ability to communicate symbolically in ways which show a change from 'domain-specific' to 'cognitive fluid' thinking.

Domain specific thought occurs in a mind constituted by multiple intelli-gences. Each of the domains – such as those for social interaction [communi-cation], for manipulating objects and for interaction with the natural world – has a limited connection with others.

Neanderthals could not take what they knew about animal behaviour and combine it with their knowledge about making artefacts to design specialised hunting weapons. They could not design beads and pendants to mediate their social interactions. This would have required bringing together technological and social intelligences.

Not only could Homo Sapiens combine the different types of knowledge, but they also had the capacity to think in metaphor – a capacity that underlies the whole of science, art and religion ... The cultural environments that we humans create around ourselves are of critical importance to the elaboration – if not the origin – of cognitive fluid thought. (Mithen, 2003: 40)

What Mithen says here links well with the connectionist group of researchers: 'Individual development cannot be fully understood without understanding its evolutionary basis.' (Elman et al., 1996: 20)

When we communicate, different parts of the brain co-ordinate (gesture and movement, vision, hearing and sound, touching, feelings and emotions). This means that everything happens at once, which makes it a complicated business to try to understand how children develop their communication systems. These things happen in co-ordination with each other. Children are constantly finding out:

- how objects and their own bodies move;
- where they begin and end, and who they are (self concept);
- what spoken/signed language is all about;
- how to co-ordinate knowledge about objects and the material world, cultural understanding, symbol making and social relationships.

Cracking the language code

Karmiloff-Smith (1992) and Goswami (1998: 278) both suggest that Piaget, who did most of his ground-breaking work between the 1930s and 1950s, was right to emphasize that children have powerful learning mechanisms. 'The mechanisms that drive children to make coherent sense of the world also lead them to pay attention to the words they hear and to learn how to use those words themselves.' (Gopnik et al., 1999: 127)

Learning to speak is like cracking a secret code. Children are investigators and experiment with language as they learn about what it is and how it works. Cracking the language code is easier if we are doing interesting things, and can talk about them together.

Learning a language is about co-ordination

Unless babies and young children are talked with and encouraged to communicate with people, they fail to develop spoken or signed language that can be used and understood by others. Gopnik et al. (1999: 101) take the view that 'Learning a language is about co-ordinating what you do with what other people do.'

Babies are 'citizens of the world' (Gopnik et al., 1999: 106) because they start life able to discriminate between the different sounds of different languages. However, as usually they are exposed to one or two languages at the most, their brains quite literally alter, and they begin to hear sound differently, so that they can no longer discriminate the finer differences. Japanese and English speakers hear the sounds 'l' and 'r' quite differently. Babies move from being what Gopnik et al. (1999: 106) call universal linguists to being 'culture-bound language specialists'.

Bilingual and multilingual children developing communication

Monolingual speakers often think that it is not normal to speak more than one language. Whitehead (2002) points out that nothing could be less true. In fact, in most parts of the world children learn to speak more than one language. Often one language is used at home, referred to by linguists as the mother tongue. Other languages are additional.

Official documents often refer to English as an additional language. However, some children are balanced bilinguals or even multilingual from the start. This means they can think in different ways about the same idea. For example, there are more words to describe different types of snow in the Inuit language than there are in English. They can more easily appreciate different forms of music, cadences and rhythms because their brains have remained open to a wider variety of sounds.

The way we relate to children who are bilingual matters. We can help them or hinder their progress according to what we do. Clarke (1992) points out that learning a new language means that children need to become familiar with new sounds and intonation patterns; new words; new ways of putting the words together; new kinds of non-verbal communication with subtle differences and meanings; different words which might be seen as rude in another language. They also need to learn a different culture introduced through learning a new language and understand how people feel and express themselves in a new language.

The way adults and children communicate

The way conversations take place has a huge influence on the richness of language development. Gopnik et al. (1999) suggest that adults almost seem to be designed to help children develop spoken or signed language.

A supportive atmosphere affects the way young children begin to use language for socializing, thinking, sharing and exchanging ideas, and talking about feelings and their relationships with others. Susan felt able to chat with Sue at Greengables because there is an atmosphere in which adults talk with children with warmth and affection. Children develop a sense of trust that they will be respected, valued and listened to. (See page 74)

The limbic system and language development

Research suggests that alterations in the development of the limbic system may occur in those children who are belittled, laughed at, ignored, or spoken at rather than with. Martin Teicher at Harvard University (2002: 54) says that 'the limbic system plays a pivotal role in the regulation of emotion and memory'.

The amygdala helps us to remember how we felt on previous similar situations, such as angry or fearful, or joyous, and leads to aggressive (and other) responses. Teicher thought that too much stress during the early years might cause long-term damage to the developing limbic system 'through excessive exposure to stress hormones' (2002: 56), suggesting that early stress 'is a toxic agent that interfered with the normal, smoothly orchestrated progressions of brain development' (2002: 61).

When young children are ignored and not listened to, or ridiculed and shouted at and punished for the things they say or made to repeat phrases they do not fully understand as part of being punished, such as 'I am sorry' or 'Thank you', they gradually, in Teicher's view (2002: 61), develop a limbic system which keeps them on heightened alert ready to react quickly and aggressively with 'robust stress responses that facilitate recovery from injury. In this sense we can reframe the brain changes we observed as adaptations to an adverse environment'.

Creating an atmosphere conducive for language learning

The tone of voice we use, the body language that accompanies what we say, the way we look at children, and the warmth and affection children receive will open them up to the kind of conversations that develop their learning about managing and expressing their feelings, thinking at deeper levels, and explaining and extending their ideas. Children who are constantly criticized, thwarted, frustrated and left without the support of conversations which help them to explore ideas or resolve problems are difficult children, angry and unhappy. They are quick to be aggressive and to take things badly because through the experiences they have had they have developed 'robust stress responses' as self-protection against feeling guilty, humiliated and angry.

Memory in developing language learning

We have seen that short-term memories help children to make on-the-spot decisions. Long-term memories help us to know more, and memories and being able to talk about them form a complex part of the development of learning.

Semantic memory

This is the way that we begin to remember and talk about:

- facts
- events
- places
- words
- objects
- concepts
- people.

Bendall (2003: 1) says that semantic memory is 'like a filing system which allows us to store and retrieve information efficiently'.

Episodic memory

Through our episodic memories we are able to reach back through our lives to recall and replay our personal life histories. Bendall (2003: 2) explains that 'It is often described as a snapshot system, because events happen only once and the memory has to be created in one go'.

As the memory is rehearsed and repeated in the hippocampus, it is gradually transferred to the more recently evolved outer layers of the neo-cortex, probably during sleep.

The importance of sleep

We often hear adults say they find it difficult to think straight and get the words out when they are tired. This is even more true for young children.

Throughout this book we see that it is important to emphasize that developing learning of all kinds should be in a healthy setting, with good nutrition, sufficient sleep, and outdoor learning and fresh air bringing oxygen to the brain.

How to develop good conversations with children

The tone of voice we use when we talk to children, the authenticity, genuineness and sincerity of our interest in the things they say, the attention we give to their attempts to put into words their ideas, feelings and relationships, are of central importance if young children are to develop into people who:

- are prepared to discuss problems;
- find ways forward through discussing and sharing solutions, and trying things out together, discussing as they do so;
- develop and deepen ideas and thoughts, putting them into words or signs;
- develop, communicate and deepen relationships with family and friends;
- are able to deal with and be confident in new situations with new people, and are able to talk things through;
- relate constructively and discuss issues and ideas with those they work with in formal relationships;
- are able to observe and tune into the non-verbal communication of others with sensitivity;
- have the confidence to try out new words, and invent words using their creativity to express their ideas, feelings and relationships;
- develop declarative (semantic and episodic) memories useful for developing language learning.

Developing language for depth of thought, feeling and relating to others

If solid communication is to develop into high-level thinking and help us to manage our feelings, both non-verbal and spoken or signed aspects need to be strong. In order for this to become part of a rich quality of living, children need to spend time with adults who pay attention to the atmosphere they create of warmth, affection, and who send the messages 'you matter' and 'what you say is interesting and important'. They need adults who listen to their attempts to put their ideas, feelings and relationships into words or signs, who talk or sign with them and not at them and who use a tone of voice which opens up the brain for learning, rather than closing learning down and placing the brain on heightened alert in an adverse environment (a chemical reaction). Children also need to be with and communicate with children older and younger than them.

Procedural memory – knowing what to do

In the nursery class of St Francis Primary School, Laurence and Sommer find themselves together at the sewing table. Nothing is said at first. Each finds and uses the materials they want, and the girl drops a piece on the floor. She finds it difficult to thread a button. The boy shows her how he does it. He turns his body towards her, and in so doing non-verbally communicates his willingness to share his knowledge. The sewing table offers children materials, embroidery frames, thread, scissors, needles and collage tray with buttons, beads, ribbons and sequins.

In many cultures of the world knowledge is taught by showing and doing, not by telling and writing. This is particularly true for learning the techniques of craft and technology. This kind of learning, which involves doing something repeatedly, such as threading a button, weaving or riding a bike is rarely forgotten once learnt. It involves procedural memories.

Shared sustained thinking

When people form close relationships of warmth and affection, which are of great importance in opening up the kind of communication which results in developing learning, there is often little speech or signing.

Concentrating – shared sustained thinking at the sewing table

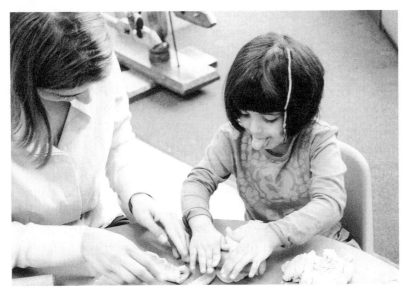

A girl in the nursery class at Prestonfield Primary School shows how she enjoys using the coloured dough. Her tongue hangs out in her concentration. She needs to be near the teacher, or her confidence vanishes when she tries new things. Her teacher gets down to her level, so that eye contact is easy. She frequently seeks eye contact, followed by a reassured smile. English is an additional language, and so non-verbal communication is even more important for her in establishing a warm relationship with the teacher. The teacher is near, but does not crowd her. She uses the dough in a reassuring side by side at first, and gradually begins to talk about what they are doing together.

Adults who tune into the child's agenda and have sensitive non-verbal communication usually find that spoken or signed language develops easily, because the child trusts them, feels valued and respected and enjoys a chat.

These kinds of thinking and conversation were identified in the continuation of EPPE study (2002) as deeply beneficial in developing the learning of young children. 'We found that the most effective settings encourage "sustained shared thinking", but we also found that this does not happen very frequently.' (Siraj-Blatchford et al., 2002: 10)

Developing spoken or signed language

After the Revolution in Nicaragua in 1979, a group of deaf children were brought together in a special residential school in Managua. When they met there they had only a few idiosyncratic and personal signs, as they had grown up as one isolated person living at home in a hearing community. As they spent time together, a natural development occurred. They began to develop a pidgin language. This was a basic language pooling the signs they had developed, which gave them the means for the first time in their lives to share ideas and feelings and communicate with each other more fully.

Pidgin and creole languages

The older teenagers continued to use this language, but the youngest children developed it until what the linguists call a creole language emerged out of the pidgin language. This was a fully fledged sophisticated sign language, unique in the world with its own grammar and a rich vocabulary of words. Kegl (1997), who researched this process, argues convincingly that humans are genetically predisposed to develop grammatical language systems. These children did just that, out of nothing.

However, there are socio-cultural aspects to her findings. Both the basic pidgin language and the sophisticated creole language had taken in elements of gestures used in the Nicaraguan culture. The children had transformed these in a more developed form into the vocabulary of the language. Also, when Kegl visited deaf children in rural areas, who were living at home without contact with other deaf children, they only used primitive gestures and signs with no grammatical element. When she introduced the children to each other, and taught them the full creole form of the sign language, the young children quickly took it up and became fluent.

This means that having a genetic predisposition for language development is not enough for a human to have. Language can only develop in the company of other people. We need to participate in our culture and language. It is not as simple as adults teaching children to talk. We need to remember that the young children in Managua taught the teenagers and adult teachers the creole, which was a more sophisticated language.

The time-scale for spoken or signed language development

There is a time-scale for language development. We have seen that language development is possible for the first decade of life, but the door begins to creak shut, and the optimum time for language development is the first five years. The wonderful thing is that there is a 'robust drive among human beings to communicate their thoughts as rapidly and efficiently as possible' (Elman et al., 1996: 390). We might add that the natural tendency to talk about feelings is not so strong. There are evolutionary reasons for this, but in a modern world talking about feelings is becoming more important if children are to develop positive and constructive relationships with others, and to develop good self-esteem, well-being and emotional literacy.

General communication and specific spoken or signed language

Some aspects of development are all-pervading and influence everything we do. Communication is of this general kind of development. Other aspects of development are quite specific and specialist in purpose and functioning. Language development is of this kind.

When humans need to develop specialisms (such as talking in a particular language, or using sign language), there is a longer period for development. Where every human needs to be able to do the same things, such as use binocular vision, the time-scale in which the development needs to be triggered by interactive experience through the senses or interactions with people tends to be shorter.

There is another difference between developments that are general to humans and those that are specific and according to cultural context. Binocular vision does not continue to develop in the way that communication and language can keep changing and adjusting.

The sounds of languages

During the first year of life babies spend huge amounts of energy organizing sound, especially sounds made by human voices. During the first three months they learn how a conversation works, with you making a sound and me replying, or the other way round.

Once they have sorted that out, they go in for experiments with babble, whole strings of consonants muh, muh, muh, buh, buh, buh (voiced and unvoiced) duh, huh, guh, using different parts of the mouth in different positions as they do so. They vary the pitch, tone and rhythm and you can almost see them listening to the results with interest. They do the same with vowel sounds. Dunn (1988) observed the pleasure babies show when adults or other children and babies echo and repeat these. Gradually, these turn, quite naturally, into what Trevarthen (1998) calls proto-conversations.

Until they are 6–8 months old babies seem to be able to distinguish between the different sounds of the world's languages. Holt, (in Gibbs, 2002: 14) at Carnegie Mellon University, counted at least 558 consonants, 260 vowels and 51 diphthongs. After this period of time, the brain specializes in the languages used by the child. English-speakers only use 52 sounds of speech (phonetic categories). Gibbs (2002: 14) suggests that, apart from the rare cases of completely balanced bilingual learning, the first language we hear influences and constrains the way we hear all other languages.

From being universal linguists to being language specialists

The longer we live, the more we can only hear the sounds of the languages we are used to. Our sense of hearing (auditory systems) becomes tuned and sensitive only to the details of the languages we speak. Babies move from being what Gopnik et al. (1999) call 'citizens of the world', or generalists capable of speaking any language, to being narrow specialists in a few languages, or even becoming monolingual. Once they are babbling at full pelt, they are narrowing into the sounds of the language or languages people speak to them.

Iverson, (in Gibbs, 2002: 14) speaking at a Conference of the Acoustical Society (2002), has come to the view that 'When you try to learn a second language, those tunings may be inappropriate and interfere with your ability to learn the new categories'. We have seen, as Gopnik et al. (1999) argue, that we naturally use what we know to learn more, using other people to help us. Most of the time this is an advantage.

Developing play supporting developing language

We will see below how it helps children to learn through the flexibility opened up in play or in the general possibilities to engage in progressive layerings of symbol use and representational behaviours. Where developing language is concerned, as Blakemore (2001) suggests, this is a disadvantage if children are brought up as monolinguals or use languages with similar roots. When children talk to themselves with small-world play scenarios, or are engaged in social dramatic play with other children and adults, language is being encouraged to take deep root.

Keeping the facility to learn new and different languages

Children who learn from an early age to speak hugely contrasting languages such as English, Urdu, Japanese or Yoruba, keep a facility to learn new languages. The research suggests that this is because they stay tuned and sensitive to more than the 52 sounds of the English language. One reason why English-speakers seem to have particular difficulty learning other languages may be that English uses such a narrow range of sounds. Another reason is that English is a dominant language in the world. This is because it was the main language of the British empire, and is now part of the American global influence.

Proto-conversations

One of the great joys of life is to have a proto-conversation with a baby. Trevarthen (1998) has helped us to value these non-verbal conversations, which use many aspects of non-verbal communication, and which form the foundations of later conversations with spoken words or signs. Non-verbal communication is possible from birth, and continues throughout our lives. Its nuances and subtle signals vary from family to family, and from culture to culture.

Even at three months old a baby will initiate a conversation with the 'coo' sound, or reply when an adult makes such sounds in a conversational tone

(Murray and Andrews, 2000). At the Castlebrae Community Centre a mother is talking to her baby in the language Trevarthen calls 'motherese'. Women and men talking to babies quite naturally speak in motherese or fatherese, and use a higher than usual voice. In the photograph on p.17, the mother pauses to give her baby the possibility to reply. She looks into his eyes, and has her eyes wide open as she speaks. She moves with the same rhythms as the baby, and they almost seem to dance together, in tune with one another's rhythms.

As babies develop into toddlers and young children, and learn more about communicating with others and themselves, their body language and hand gestures become more sophisticated. The body can be tense and anxious, in an alert pose, move with total joy, flail about in anger, restless with boredom, totally absorbed and not open to distraction. It is helpful when adults help them to be aware of their own and other people's non-verbal communications.

'Oh, you've bumped your leg. I can see it's hurting you. Your face is showing me.'

Pauses and turn-taking can be encouraged if adults listen to what children say as much as they expect children to listen to what they say. Conversations are two-way. Many studies (Wells, 1987) of so-called conversations between adults and children show that adults often deliver speeches, or insist on their ideas being the focus, or ask questions they know the answers to. In real conversations no one knows exactly the twists and turns the conversation will take, which keeps interest alive for those taking part. It takes two to talk. If one person dominates and has most of the say, it is not much of a conversation.

Scaffolding the language learning – Bruner

Following the findings from research that show that adults tend to dominate by talking at children, attempts were made to address this using the notion of scaffolding developed from Vygotsky's work (1978) by Bruner (1977).

Bruner (1977) argued that adults act as if the child had intentions. When scaffolding, the adult tunes into the unspoken intention of the child by observing how the child tackles a task. However, the adult has it in mind to help her or him understand how to make the characters and storyline of a play scenario.

At Prestonfield Nursery class, a girl makes the small dolls walk about, and seems to intend to make up characters in a story about the seaside. She makes a small-world play scenario out of them.

The adult makes the doll talk in a high voice, and suggests she wants to make a sand-castle. The adult puts into words the unspoken, intention of the child and makes it become more conscious, and more available as a future strategy to be used in play. In this way the teacher extends her understanding of how to develop both a character and a storyline by providing one. However, this is not the child's story. It is the adult's attempt to lead the child into making a story with a character in it.

Scaffolding is about adults tutoring towards an adult-led and adult-identified piece of learning. It has an important part to contribute in developing learning.

It is very different from free-flow play, which makes its contribution to learning in a different way. In free-flow play, neither the child nor the adult knows where they will land up. The adult goes where the child goes, helping him or her along their way, as Holland (2003: 54) does in this play scenario.

> *I was welcomed wholeheartedly into the game, a reception I would not necessarily expect if children were absorbed in free flow dramatic play, and my suggestion that we should go hunting for the 'flat monsters' I'd heard were hiding under the sofa was received with relish. I hinted that surprise was of the essence and this resulted in four boys crawling and slithering silently across the room to peer under the sofa … . The boys embraced the scenario: some got nasty flat monster bites and needed urgent treatment. Others spotted the monsters escaping and trying to steal the Batmobile.*

Because free-flow play arises spontaneously, it has to be helped during the flowing, which is now. The adult has to seize the moment, and tune into the children's play agenda of the flat monsters there and then, acting as a skiful opportunitst, and in doing so helping the boys to take the characters and story further.

Just as Siraj-Blatchford et al. (2002: 10) observed that 'shared sustained thinking was not frequently observed', so it is in my observations in a variety of settings, that only a few skilled practitioners seem to join free-flow play and develop it without destroying or invading it.

Vygotsky – meaning imparted by others

Vygotsky (1978) suggests that children develop meaning because other people impart meaning to what they do. When a child tries to grab a cup, without success, the adult often gives him or her the cup, and says, 'Do you want a drink?'

This gives meaning to the general grabbing movements natural in a young child, and so the child begins to point at objects they want with intention. Children learn how to use a cultural object, like a cup, as a way of communicating with people.

Piaget, Vygotsky and Bruner

Piaget, Bruner and Vygotsky agree that the development of intention is important and is deeply linked with the development of language learning. However, they disagree about the way that intention develops.

Piaget thought that children used the cup as a way of reaching an end during the sensory motor period. By pointing at the cup, the child could get the adult to give him or her a drink he or she could not reach. In this way the child gets the drink he or she wants and gets the attention of the adult.

Bruner favours a view that the adult tutors the child by acting 'as if' the child has an intention to get the cup, although Bruner sees the child as too immature to have an awareness of their intention. Bruner agrees with Piaget that the child has a goal, but it is incipient, although it involves both the cup and the person who will help. This contrasts with Vygotsky, who thought the child made an unsuccessful grasping movement for the cup which brought a reaction from the adult. Other people give meaning to what the child does, which leads the child to have this as an intention (getting the cup).

In a way it does not matter which explanation is correct, because Vygotsky, Bruner and Piaget agree in the description of what happens. Children point at things, and adults assume they are interested in what they point at, and talk to them about this, and often give them the objects they point at. As Vila (in Tryphon and Voneche, 1996: 192–4) says, the 'views coincide'. This is an example, not so much of converging evidence, but of an area of solidarity between these theories.

With time, toddlers, young children and adults enjoy joint attention and talk about something or an event that they both focus on together.

In practice

- Is your setting rich in communication? Look at your displays. What do they tell people about the values and principles pervading the setting?
- Do the notice-boards give important messages about inclusion, diversity and information exchange? How do you make children and families feel they belong? How do you show them that you see them as individuals?
- How easy is it for parents and carers to communicate and dialogue with staff?
- How good at observation are you? Do you note the subtle forms of non-verbal communication which inform you about a child's feelings, ideas or physical well-being, for instance the intensity of focus when using paint, the tearfulness when they have to wait for a turn on a bike? The way you observe and act on your observations will lead to rich (or poor) communication between you and that child.
- Do you value non-verbal communication? Do you set up areas with workshops for three- and two-dimensional art, dancing, music, looking for beetles in the garden, splashing in puddles, cuddling in for a one-to-one story? What the child chooses to do communicates how he or she feels, thinks and relates to others.

Further reading

Bruce, T. and Meggitt, C. (2002) *Childcare and Education*, 3rd edn, Chapter 5. London: Hodder and Stoughton.

Manolson, A. (1992) *It Takes Two to Talk: A Parent's Guide to Helping Children to Communicate*. Toronto, Ontario: Hanen Centre.

Peters, C. (2002) 'Communication', *Early Childhood Practice: The Journal for Multi-Professional Partnerships* 4(1): 41–50.

6

Talk

Key themes

We can only learn to talk or sign if we are with other people.

Language and making meaning go together. When we do not understand the words we use, we are held back in our learning. This is why learning words empty of meaning does not remain with us.

We learn to talk most effectively when we are not feeling under pressure to perform. Then we can think straight, and the words come tumbling out. It is the same for children and adults. We need to be with people who are interested in our efforts to try to put ideas, thoughts, feelings and relationships into words or signs. When people are sensitive in the way they do this, everyone begins to talk in ways which lead to deeper conversations. We ponder on the what, why, when and where aspects of our lives. We begin to muse and ask questions. We make more of our experiences of life. We develop our learning together.

Oscar Wilde (in Pinker, 1995: 19) is quoted as remarking that 'It is well to remember from time to time that nothing that is worth knowing can be taught'. A theme of this book is that we need to develop learning carefully, and that this requires great skill and sensitivity from adults. The best teaching is often indirect, and those observing may not realize it is happening because it is so subtle. Sophisticated and skilled teaching of this kind is often not appreciated by those who do not understand the complexities of learning.

Pinker (1995: 56) sees language development as what he calls a 'discrete combinatorial system'. This means that the language system in our brains can make infinite use of finite media. Grammar and speech sounds form the finite media. These can be formed into infinite combinations in the different languages of the world.

Rich language develops out of shared experiences with those who know how to talk fluently. Steels (2002: 2), working with robots at the SONY Computer Science Laboratory in Paris, has come to the view that language: 'particularly in its earliest phases, develops out of shared experiences, and so has to be grounded in the real world. In other words there has to be something to talk about.'

In no way does Steels suggest that the robots are learning language as humans do, but he does believe that language and meaning co-evolve. The two are intimately linked. Karmiloff-Smith (1992: 69) points out that children are both problem-solvers and problem-generators. She, like Steels, argues that children put enormous effort into meaning-making. They invent language as well as take in the language spoken to them.

'It's roundy, roundy. Look'

At Greengables, two girls are experimenting with oil and paint in the water tray. They chat to each other about what is happening. 'Mine's going round – and round – and round.' 'So's mine. Look. Look at mine. It's roundy roundy. Look.'

The rules of grammar

Steels (2002: 2) looks at the development of spoken grammar in a different way from many linguists. 'It's no frustrating set of rules to be used rigidly and to be grammatically correct. It's purely to help us to understand.' Like Whitehead (2002), he sees language as constantly evolving, with words changing their meaning, new words emerging and others fading, but also with the rules and grammar changing too.

He believes that Chomsky has a static view of language, with fundamental rules of grammar common to all languages and hardwired into the brain. Steels's work with computers which talk to each other and make meaning together raises some of the age-old arguments about how human language develops. Are linguistic rules and sounds encoded in the brain and genes, as Chomsky suggested? Or is it simply a matter of learning the rules, as the behavioural psychologists, such as Barrhus Frederic Skinner, thought? He did not think it was useful to theorize about mental states that could not be observed. It looks as if the answer is neither.

Instead, language is a complex interaction, through which babies from birth begin a lifelong process of what Calvin (1996: 88) calls 'intelligent guessing', as we communicate with ourselves and others and generate ideas. Intelligent guessing helps young children to listen to words and grammar and make sense that way. Intelligent inventing of language, using what they hear as best they can, helps them to speak. Speaking and listening go along together and help each other.

Developing language by talking and listening

Developing as monolinguals, bilinguals or multilinguals

Babies meet the huge challenge of having to find out what language is about. Children who are born with profound hearing loss or with complex needs have an even greater challenge in front of them. However, once babies and children have worked out how to invent language and crack the codes of different languages, a whole new world of opportunity opens up.

Whitehead, some of whose grandchildren are bilingual, explains the pleasure of seeing how children reveal what they understand about language as they become emergent speakers. Bilingual children regularly switch from one language to another, and they mix the two languages. They are certainly not demonstrating muddled thinking when they do this. Instead they are showing us some very effective strategies they are using to build bridges from one language to another.

Trying out language

It is important that children are encouraged to try out a new language, or indeed their developing first language, free from pressure, without too much public attention. We have seen that as adults we have an important role to play in the way we have conversations with children singly or in small groups. Huge groups, when children are herded together, are not relaxed places for language or any other kind of learning. Indeed, language is inhibited and discouraged in such settings.

Children will talk more readily with one other interested, sensitive person, or sometimes, when appropriate, in small groups, where they feel safe to contribute, and where they do not have to constantly wait for the chance to speak. They can watch others speak, listen more easily and join in when they feel safe to do so, knowing their attempts to speak will be encouraged, and that no one will rush them, speak for them, criticize any errors or mock them.

'Sevcan (4 years old) is a relatively new pupil from Turkey, who spoke no English when she came to St. Francis School. She takes the mop to the hall area to "clean" it. The pail is by her foot, having no water in it. She uses her imagination. Sadman has lifted the brush and pan to help her. He is also learning to speak English.' (Lamb, 2001, narrative observation)

The children are communicating through play, non-verbally. They are free from pressure in making a story together, which will encourage them to try out words and phrases in English.

First words and phrases

Children do not talk in a vacuum. They need people to talk with, and interesting things to talk about. Their first words are about the people they love and important objects, such as drinking cups, spoons, pets, push-chairs or favourite toys. Both the people they talk with and the objects of their world reflect the cultural context in which they are growing up or visiting.

According to Mandler (1999), one of the first words children speak in the US is 'gone', but adults tend to miss what the child is trying to say. Instead they celebrate when children say 'Mama' or 'Dada'. She suggests that understanding of language and space develop together. The word 'gone' is the child's attempt to describe what is happening to the biscuit that falls off the high-chair, as it moves from one part of space to another.

We can see that children are learning through the senses and movement, alongside developing language and the episodic memory system, and they begin to remember the words long-term. Of course, children remember and invent words which make meaning about their feelings, relationships and ideas.

Cultivating talk

Vygotsky (1978: 118) makes the distinction between 'cultivating' and 'imposing' learning. Adults tend to talk at children. What they need to do is to talk with them, if they are going to cultivate language so that it develops richly.

> *Talking with young children is thus very much like playing ball with them. What the adult has to do for this game to be successful, is first to ensure the child is ready with arms cupped, to catch the ball. The ball must be thrown gently and accurately so that it lands in the child's arms. When it is the child's turn to throw, the adult must be prepared to run wherever it goes and bring it back to where the child really intended it to go.* (Gordan Wells, 1987: 50)

Sensitivity to what the child says

Anna Freud always believed that the best educators of young children do not require the children to follow them. They follow the children, and see each as an individual within a group.

Modern speech therapists like Manolson (1992) agree. She stresses the importance of allowing children to lead conversations. She thinks it is important for adults to share the moment with a child, and in doing so, to add language and experience. This means we need to avoid talking 'for' children because we are in a hurry. We need to tune into what the child is trying to say, or is saying without words. Then we find out how children feel and what they are thinking.

Manolson (1992) encourages adults to work in the following ways.

- Be face to face, and not to loom over children. (Bend the knees, get down on the floor, lie on your tummy, sit on the floor and give the child a chair.)
- Show that you are listening by echoing the baby's sounds, or by repeating what they have said. It's a flower, yes, a beautiful yellow flower.

- Interpret by guessing what the child has said if it is unclear, and use a questioning tone, or explain that you don't understand gently and encourage the child to keep trying different ways to communicate until you understand. Oh. You bumped your head. It hurts, does it? Rub it to help it stop hurting.
- Be a good turn taker. You cannot have a conversation unless you take turns with the child.
- Keep the conversation going. Tune into the child's non-verbal communication with you. Expand what you talk about.

When adults are sensitive to children's interests, children want to be with them

The last item, keeping the conversation going, is a real challenge to adults working with children to support their language development in ways which are right for each child. Some children have their own ideas, and are not eager to share them. Some love to talk to you. Some children are shy, while others, for one reason or another, have become withdrawn. Some chat away as they go, but do not pause to really engage in a good chat about something they will focus on.

Having interesting experiences to talk about

At Children's House, Nickie is sewing. He is supported in this by the staff member. She gets down to his level, and really listens to him as he tries to explain that the thread is tangling. She shows him that he needs to go in one side of the material and come out the other side. He needs her to keep reminding him of this.

She does not overwhelm him with two many teaching points. She focuses on one. She has chosen to talk about this with him because he has shown her and tried to tell her that this is his frustration. In this way, she helps him to succeed. He keeps going, with her support, and is free to choose his design. They discuss the choices he (not she) makes, as they go chatting along together.

Asking children questions

Asking children questions is a hazardous business. Questions only help language development and the development of shared sustained thinking and conversations if the adult genuinely wants to know the answer, and is sincere. Most questions we ask children are not of that sort.

Manolson (1992: 21) suggests that appropriate, sincere questions might:

- help children to anticipate. What next? What if? What now?
- allow children to choose and decide. Do you want to paint or to use the clay?
- extend a child's thinking. What's happening? How does it work?

One of the first people to take a long deep look at children's questions was Nathan Isaacs (in Isaacs, 1930: 291) the scientist husband of Susan Isaacs. He looked at the 'why' questions of four-year-olds. He had the emphasis right. Questions are only useful to children in developing their learning if they act as a starting-point for further investigation. They are a hopeless waste of time and energy when they become a way for adults to indulge in question-and-answer sessions. When questions are authentic, and act as a beginning of some kind of investigation, they are a valuable way of making conversations rich.

Questions from adults often become part of a power relationship (sometimes called hegemony) in which the adult holds all the power. When this happens, the adults ask questions to which they know the answers, and dismiss the children's questions, musings and queries as off-task.

Questions helping us to get in touch with other people's minds

The first year or so of life is typically spent developing some key words and phrases which help children to 'exchange meaning' and begin the 'complex business of getting two minds in contact', according to Whitehead (2002: 4). Once these are used spontaneously by the child, and recognized by family or carers and used with consistency, an explosion of language usually follows. 'What?' is followed by questions about when, where, how and why.

Questions helping children to see reason

We have seen that children are concerned from the start with words and talk about events in space, but the questions which develop from about two years of age show us that they are also fascinated by time, the reasons for things and what causes what to happen, because time as well as objects, space and reasons affect the way people act.

Learning to talk is as emotional as it is intellectual. Where Mummy has gone, when she will return, and why she went are events full of feeling. The investigations around answering these questions show how we can help children to face, deal with and manage their feelings if we support their thinking and help them to understand and talk about things in an intellectual way. 'Knowledge is continually restructured and revised in the light of experience.' (Goswami, 1998: 281)

Questions do not have to be attached to question marks. Saying 'I wonder', 'What if', 'Supposing' are other forms of question which also open up investigation and reflection for children.

Encouraging children to question

The best help adults can give to children is to help them to begin to ask their own questions, and to share their investigations and thinking through the 'shared sustained conversations' identified by Siraj-Blatchford (2002) as so important in developing learning.

> At the Castlebrae family centre Christopher observed June, the nursery nurse, making the bread. 'What you do, June?' On being told that she was making bread for snack, he said, 'Me help you'. He followed instructions and kept a small piece of dough to make a roll for himself. (observation by Lyn Tarlton)

Through the question he asks June, Christopher knows about what will happen to the dough. He can move away from the present and into the future: bread. This knowledge helps him to bring more understanding to what needs to be done with the dough, now, in the present.

First-hand, real experience is vital for the development of language. Sharing experiences together cultivates language, because it is through real experience that children begin to make sense of their learning and to understand what people are saying to them. In Chapter 7, we shall look in detail at the way that children learn through their senses and through movement.

How adults are crucial

Unless children have real experiences which help them to understand the meaning of what people say to them, they do not speak and develop their talk. They depend on adults and other children in this. Adults are crucial in giving them added information.

When a child finds a bead that shines and shows it to us, we can share the moment by talking about it with him or her. A child will be eager to listen and take part because we are adding information about the bead. If the child drops the bead, we can say, 'Oops, did you see it bounce?' This adds vocabulary in a real situation. He or she will probably want to make it bounce again, and you can talk about it together. If the child then begins to throw the bead, you can say, 'It's fine to bounce the bead on the floor, but if you throw it, it might go in someone's eye, so I can't let you do that.'

Extending the conversation – increasing the vocabulary

Children can only increase their vocabulary if they are with people who offer them new words during the conversation.

- Naming. That's a car.
- Emphasizing the key word. That's a *car*.
- Explaining. Daddy goes to work in the car.
- Talking about feelings. You like going in the car, don't you?
- Describing. That car is very dirty.

- Pretending. Let's push the chair and pretend it's a car.
- Talking about what you did yesterday, or in the recent past.
- Talking about the future. Tomorrow we are going to Grandma's house in the car.

All the time that we are talking with children, we are using gesture, body language, facial expressions and other kinds of non-verbal communication. In this way we show children how we feel as we shake our head to say 'No'.

Some thoughts for an adult who wishes to support children's language development would be:

- If I say something, will you notice?
- If I say something, will you reply?
- Will we want to say more to each other?
- What will we talk about?

As we saw above, what we talk about with children is of deep importance. There is nothing like a really fascinating conversation between people, when each can contribute and develop their thoughts and feelings about something which interests everyone. Siraj-Blatchford et al. (DFES, 2002) shows that 'shared sustained thinking' and conversations make a huge contribution to the learning of young children (and probably throughout our lives). Children with a narrow vocabulary at three or four years of age are at a disadvantage as readers and writers, or in managing their own behaviour at the end of primary school.

Being cut off from talking with others is a major setback. It occurs, for instance, when people have strokes and lose speech; are unable to speak the language of others; and are isolated from others.

Rich language gives richness of quality in thinking, understanding, managing feelings, socializing and relating to others, and in the sense of embodiment.

In practice

- Do you take the time to talk with children? When you are rushing about focusing on the organizational side of the work, you might not be stopping to think why you are here. Remind yourself that you are here to make children's lives as rich as you can.
- When children approach you, do you get down to eye level with them, and listen and say something worth saying back, or do you just make a quick, polite reply and move on quickly?
- Do you follow up conversations with children? 'You know you showed me the model aeroplane you made, and I said it reminded me of a bi-plane, well, I found one in this book.'
- Do you follow up what interested a child, or do you follow up what interested you? You might find that you help children to learn more if you begin with what the child finds fascinating.
- Do you find that when you help one child to learn by following his or her interest, it spreads and gathers in other children?
- Do you find that when your observations of children are used to inform the planning you do with colleagues, your plans are much better, and everyone enjoys learning more?

Further reading

Clarke, P. (1992) *English as a Second Language in Early Childhood*. Victoria, Australia: Free Kindergarten Association.

Rice, S. (2001) 'Luke's Story', *Early childhood Practice: The Journal for Multi-Professional Partnerships* 3(2): 60–8.

Whitehead, M. (1990) 'First Words. The Language Diary of a Bilingual Child's Early Speech', *Early Years* 10(2): 3–14.

Whitehead, M. (2002) *Developing Language and Literacy with Young Children*, 2nd edn. London: Paul Chapman Publishing.

7

Doing real things

Key themes

It is important for children to learn to use their senses to the full. The most effective learning occurs when children are offered rich, broad and deep experiences which encourage them to use sight, sound, movement, touch, taste and smell in co-ordination. Woodwork, cookery, sand and water, and opportunities to climb and balance are important parts of the early childhood curriculum.

Learning is developed naturally through the preparation and sharing of meals, and also through the active learning that takes place in a well-structured learning environment, both indoors and outdoors.

When this happens, it does not matter whether a child is a visual, kinaesthetic or whatever learner! There is something for every kind of learning, and so all children can be included and gain access to learning. All children benefit from multi-sensory learning and feedback from their movements.

Adults are of central importance in carefully structuring the learning environment (the material, timings of the day, routines, ways of offering experiences and materials, sensitive conversations).

Children are more likely to remember learning that is actively using the senses.

Developing the senses and movement

Sight

At the beginning of this book we met Christopher. We noted that as he looked around him on his journey in the push-chair to the Castlebrae Family Centre, he used his well-established binocular vision. This means that he could see what was around him in clear images, with both his eyes co-ordinating.

103

Hearing

He can do something equivalent with both his ears. He can work out where sounds are in space. This is called sound location. Ratey (2001: 94) says, 'The ability to detect the spatial location of sounds is a profound evolutionary advancement.'

Our interacting senses

Of course, the ways in which we hear or see things are not isolated events. 'The senses interact to create a world that, well, 'makes sense' to us. Researchers have found that linguistic visual cues, such as the shape of the lips, activate the auditory cortex, while facial movements that are not identifiable as speech do not.' (Ratey, 2001: 95)

Our brains also allow us to pick out important sound amid a cacophony of sound. We can hear what someone near us is saying, even in a crowded room full of noise and music. We are very tuned into to human voices. Indeed, it is true to say that we seem, at times, to hear with our eyes, and see with our ears. All our senses (seeing, hearing, tasting, smelling, touching) and feedback from the movements we make are connected, co-ordinating and working together.

Movement

Young children learn through their senses and feedback from movements, but only if the environment is supportive. The development of learning is seriously constrained and may be long-term damaged when young children are placed in bare classrooms with mainly paper and pencil exercises led by adults, there are long periods of sitting still, and adults do most of the talking and require children to follow their adult set tasks.

Goddard-Blythe (2000: 7) states that sitting still requires great co-ordination, even for adults. Any adult who has experienced a back problem will know this.

Touch

This is the first sense to develop (Ratey, 2001: 76). 'The rooting reflex, the most primitive early sign of touch, occurs when a baby turns its head toward a mother's hand when she touches his face. It helps the newborn baby locate its mother's nipple when it is feeding. Infants respond instinctively to other forms of tactile stimulation. For instance, if you touch an infant's hand she will grip your finger tightly. Tickle her foot and she will curl her toes.'

Premature babies and touch

Field's study (1999) showed that when premature babies were massaged for 15 minutes three times each day, they gained 47 percent more weight than other premature babies.

Babies and children deprived of physical touch

The swaddled babies found by Mary Carlson in the Romanian orphanages were never touched, but propped up to be fed. All aspects of their development were stunted, so that they seemed to be half their age.

Ratey (2001: 78), who is an American, is concerned that children shown little physical affection are more likely to become violent as adults. American children receive less physical affection than children in many other countries. He gives evidence that, for example in France a friend will touch a shoulder or hand of a friend 200 times in half an hour, while in the US, children do this, on average, only twice in the same time.

Taste

Taste and food go together, as we shall see below in the 'Food for Tot' project (pp. 121–4).

We have taste buds on the tongue; in our cheeks; in the roof of the mouth; and in the throat.

The four primary tastes which have become important as humans have evolved are:

- sweetness, our search for energy;
- saltiness, which maintains body fluids and electrolyte balance;
- sourness, warns against spoiled food;
- bitterness, guards against toxins and poisons.

The Japanese have a fifth sense, *umami*, which means 'delicious' and 'yummy'.

Because of neurogenesis, we can continuously repair our sense of taste when it is damaged by drinking a very hot or very cold drink, or scraping our tongue.

Eating food

When we have a cold, we cannot smell what we taste, and so our food seems to be flavourless. Taste and smell go together. We feel the touch (texture and temperature) of food as we eat it, using our tongue. Very hot or very cold drinks dull our taste buds.

The way food looks and is presented is important. The sound of crockery, cutting, the clink of glasses, all add to the meal-time experience.

Below we shall look at practical ways of involving children in daily food preparation and eating together in a relaxed way, which encourages 'yummy' mealtimes in enjoyable company.

Learning through the senses and movement

Learning through the senses and movement means active learning, which means that children are encouraged to have intellectual lives in which they have to make decisions and choices, and through which they develop interests, tackle things that challenge them, with the support of others, and are prepared to persevere when the going gets tough, gaining confidence and well-being during the process.

Active learning encourages children to :

- be autonomous;
- be self-motivated;
- show courage;
- think of others;
- go deep in their learning.

This is because it supports and extends learning in ways which engage the whole child. This involves ideas, feelings, relationships and the physical side of learning. Environments which cultivate active learning through the senses and movement develop learning in all its dimensions.

Learning styles and multi-sensory approaches

Much has been written about different learning styles. These have two dimensions (Rayner and Riding, 1999: 9):

- the 'holistic-analytic' dimension, involving organizing information into wholes or parts.

- the 'verbal-imagery' dimension, in which children represent information in mental pictures as they talk and think.

This research using older children links with the work of Dennie Wolf during the 1980s with young children. She and her colleagues on the Harvard Zero Project (Wolf and Gardner, 1978) found that some toddlers preferred to use a set of play teasets as role-play props and had tea parties. Others made the teacups and saucers into patterns.

Wolf called the children dramatists (which links with the verbal-imagery dimension) and patterners (which links with the holistic-analytic dimension). However, and this is important, by three years of age, the children in the study used both learning styles with comfort. They used their preferred style to get access into the other style. So a patterner would be likely to lay the table with care before sitting teddy and dolls at the table for a tea-party. A dramatist might get the doll to lay the table and be the parent calling the children to tea.

This all adds up to saying that it does not really matter what the learning style of a child is. What matters is that the learning environment indoors and outdoors caters for all styles and uses a multi-sensory approach. This is at the heart of developing learning in any home or any setting.

Nursery schools have done this for 100 years or so in the UK, and have been emulated across the world for the quality that shines out of them. With their emphasis on outdoor and indoor environments, and active learning using the senses and movement in a supportive community, they have a sustained track record of high quality, recognized in research studies (EPPE, 2002).

In this chapter we shall see how we can make environments indoors and outdoors that cultivate the development of learning. A learning environment can be in a home or in a group setting. It needs to value the fact that some of the best learning takes place outside, and that it is rather a strange idea to think that learning is only possible indoors.

The outdoor garden

It should not matter whether a child chooses to spend time indoors or outdoors. It will only limit a child in developing learning if either the indoor or outdoor areas do not offer as much as they should. Outdoor areas often fail to offer children all that they need in order to maximize the development of their learning.

There are two different approaches to organizing the outdoor area for active (not passive) learning experiences.

Approach one: differences between indoors and outdoors

Here the opportunities for learning outside are rather different from indoors. In New Zealand, a project at Auckland College of Education (Hatherly) suggests that it is important to have:

- an open space;
- a large area for sand;
- climbing and swinging areas;
- investigating area;
- planting and nature;
- adult discussion of how it will look in ten years' time;
- natural shrubs and plants throughout the garden.

This approach emphasizes the importance of creating a state of flow between the different areas outdoors, but also from the indoor to the outdoor areas, so that everything is placed in a carefully considered way, creating a co-ordinated whole area spanning indoors and outdoors.

Approach two: resonance between indoors and outdoors

This approach, based on the traditions of British nursery schools, suggests that everything that is offered indoors should, in a different form, be offered outdoors. Ouvry stresses that the child who spends time on the climbing frame using the shoulder is developing the physical co-ordination and skill needed to write with a pencil (Ouvry, 2000). She suggests that adults should try stretching out an arm, and holding a bar on the frame, in order to see that this movement involves the pencil-holding muscles. A child might paint indoors with paint at a table, but outdoors with a bucket of water and a roller on the tarmac or walls, as in Greengables Nursery School. In this way, the outdoor garden complements and resonates with the indoor rooms.

In this book you will find examples and photographs of children climbing, swinging, planting, investigating, playing in sand and using large open spaces. You will also see children making use of outdoor areas which complement what is offered indoors. A combination of the two approaches makes a powerful result.

Woodwork, a traditional learning experience

At Cameron House Nursery School, one of the staff supports children at the woodwork bench, which is placed outside, to help with both the noise and mess of woodwork. This is active learning at its best. A girl (four years) uses the saw. She is feeling the need to be near the adult, as she gains confidence and courage.

The adult has helped her to secure the wood in a vice. The saw is appropriate for her size of hands. The wood is soft enough to saw and is not splintery. She has enough space to saw without endangering others. These are safety issues, and the adults have made careful risk assessments and shared them with parents. Rather than a focus on safety, which can lead to emphasizing danger, it is more useful to emphasize risk assessment, which leads to finding ways forward so that children are not deprived of invaluable learning experiences. There is a now 100 years of tradition of offering woodwork experience safely to young children in the UK (and other countries).

The children are provided with and shown how to use:

- a woodwork bench;
- one hammer, not too big and heavy, not too small and light;
- one hand-saw, again of a good size for a small child to hold;
- one vice in which to secure wood;
- a selection of nails in a box, stored on the shelf under the bench ;
- a pair of pliers with which to hold nails on the bench, or remove nails;
- carefully selected wood that is not splintery or too hard, stored under the bench but displayed in an attractive, accessible way;
- sandpaper stuck on to a block of wood, easily held by a child's hand;
- a template for each tool on the bench to aid tidying up time;
- a table where finished constructions or work in progress can be put.

Giving children technical vocabulary

The adult holds down the wood for a boy who is joining two bits of wood by hammering in a nail. As both children go about their different woodwork, the adult talks to them, providing words like 'hammer', and 'saw' so as to offer them the technical vocabulary of woodwork. Children depend on adults to help them increase their vocabularies in ways which help them to think and understand.

Getting to know how wood behaves

Talking together as you share an interesting experience

Just joining wood together with a hammer or sawing a piece of wood is not of the same quality as talking together about what equipment is called, what it is for and what children might make. In the first instance, children will need to get to know materials and how they behave. What does wood do? How can you transform it from one shape to another, or join bits together? What are the tools called?

As we saw in Chapter 6, children appreciate both non-verbal and spoken or signed chatting about such things. They are active learners, and want to know. The thrill of being allowed, in a safe secure way, with clear boundaries and support, to use woodwork tools when you are only three or four years old, is probably never forgotten. This is high-quality learning.

As children become more competent:

- they begin to take responsibility for safety and to make risk assessments;
- they learn how to take a nail out of the wood with the two-pronged end of the hammer;
- they make sophisticated constructions and models;
- they understand the need for axles, hinges, springs, triangles to keep the shape of rectangular models, and how to join sections;
- they learn the difference between a nail and a screw, a hammer and a screw-driver, a vice and the functions of different saws;
- they learn science and technology;
- they represent (make) things like cars, which takes children into being expressive, creative, communicative and story-makers.

Links with the areas of learning

To make links with the different areas of learning, you can look at any of the official curriculum framework documents of the UK. Rather than emphasizing what children learn, other countries tend to place more emphasis on how children learn and the dispositions important for learning, such as the Nordic countries, the New Zealand framework called *Te Whariki*, Pistoia and Reggio Emilia in Northern Italy.

It is important for those of us living in the UK to bear in mind that **how** children learn (through actively using their senses and movement, with a community of people) is as important as what children learn during the earliest years.

Process and product

Not all constructions that children make are products. They may have been experiments with wood, or clay, paint or found material, mark-making or movement and sound. It is very important that children have opportunities to find out what materials will do and how they behave. Just as it is important not to push children into making products when process is what is important in the learning, so it is important to show children you value the products they make.

Not all children want a public fuss about their efforts. They may want to take what they have made home, or to take home the photograph or video you took as they danced or made music, and share this quietly with their family or carers.

They may like to have a little chat about their product, the dance they made, the song they composed, the drawing, painting, book they made, or model or clay sculpture. They may give their permission for you to display their creation. At Children's House, a variety of wooden constructions are made into a display, and a book about wood is part of this. This encourages children into discussions about where wood comes from, and its many uses.

The fascination of glue

> *Christopher, who is two years old, had been using the glue for many months, but was not at all interested in a finished product. He enjoyed running the glue through his fingers. We provided 'gluck' as an additional sensory experience. After this he began using the glue for sticking things together, having compared the properties of both.* (Tarlton, 2002)

The adults are being active in supporting Christopher, using their observations to make individual provision for him, and also using their observations to alert them when he moves to the next point in his developing learning. He now understands what glue is for.

Understanding how to transform materials

Children use their senses to learn about materials, and they learn from feedback from their movements in relation to them (kinaesthetic learning). We have seen that children often begin to represent (make) things like cars as they experiment with different materials. More is written about representing through being a symbol user in other chapters too, as it is such a central part of being a human.

Water – What is it like?

What caused that to happen?

Another important aspect of developing learning is the way that children begin to tease out what causes something to happen. This is closely linked to understanding how things change and transform. The sand might behave in one way when it is dry, and quite differently when it is wet. How did it change and transform from the first state (dry) to the final state (wet)? What happened in between the initial state and the final state?

We tend to ban children from tipping water into dry sand on the grounds that the sand becomes smelly as it takes time to dry out. Corinne and John Hutt made a study (Hutt, Tyler, Hutt and Christopherson, 1988) which suggested that children learn a huge amount from engaging in these kinds of transformations, especially if adults help them to make sense of it all through fascinating discussions and chats (not giving lectures).

Piaget called these transformations functional dependencies. A simpler way of putting this is to say understanding transformations helps children to develop cause-and-effect relationships (Athey, 1990: 29). Children need to understand:

- the starting point (a piece of wood);
- the end result (two pieces of wood and some sawdust);
- the way that what happens in between changes the beginning into the end state of the transformation (sawing the wood, held in a vice).

Reversible and irreversible

Some transformations can be reversed. Wet sand can be dried out. The water from dissolved salt and sugar can be evaporated. Ice can be melted back into the water it started as. Steam can be condensed back into water

Some transformations cannot be reversed. Once wood is chopped up, or turned to sawdust, it cannot be a whole piece of wood or a tree again. This is why cooking with children, or having bonfires and barbecues, helps them to see how materials transform, either reversibly, or irreversibly, like burning wood or charcoal into ash. Providing proper risk assessments are made, these important childhood learning experiences can be offered. Forest schools and nursery schools are leading the way in this respect.

Getting to know the materials

However, before children can appreciate and understand transformations and cause and effect relationships, or represent things (such as dogs, people, houses, trees and cars) they will need to get to know the materials through senses and movement feedback. It is as if they are saying to themselves, 'This is sand. Is it still sand when it is in a bucket, and when it is spread out in the sand pit or sand tray? Does it always pour? Does it always sprinkle?' They are finding out that sand is sand is sand, and has certain attributes which are always present. These attributes are what we might call the 'sandness of sand'.

The 'sandness' of sand

It is quite useful for us as adults to remind ourselves of the properties and attributes of materials. What is sand? It is shells from the sea ground by the waves across time, and thrown up to form beaches. Children cannot know this unless we help them to know it. Providing children with pestle and mortar and shells and helping them to make sand is a popular thing to do. Taking children to the beach is ideal. Providing containers and spades, rakes and sieves, are all helpful, together with interesting chatting together.

Fullness, emptiness, and wet sand

A three-year-old girl at Cameron House is absorbed in her exploration of sand. Her mother does not rush her away at home time, but respects her fascination, talking with her about what she is doing. Children will not learn words and phrases about what is central to sand if we do not talk with them.

She is using a shovel, filling a bucket, but will it be full to the top? Will she empty it before she goes home? Is the spade the right size to fit in the bucket? She is scooping sand up with it. She could sprinkle the sand because it is wet, but can she pour it, or would it have to be dry?

Her mother is a good observer, and by tuning into her daughter's fascination with the sand, she establishes that she is interested in filling the bucket with the sand. She gears the conversation towards this, and so helps her daughter to investigate and develop her learning about the sand.

Making sense, children and adults together

Children do not learn everything from adults. Some people seem to think that unless adults teach children something, they cannot learn about it. There are many examples in this book of children learning from materials and from each other. Adults can sometimes hinder learning more than they help it, when they are not sensitive, informed observers who tune into what interests a child, and are skilled in using what the child knows and takes to readily as access into more challenging areas for the child.

In a sequence of photographs taken at Children's House, a group of children are involved in picking blackberries. They talk to each other and form theories about them. They are black. They are easy to squash. They grow on prickly brambles. You can eat them. You can cook them. They can make jam. They are using what they already know about blackberries from previous encounters with them, and making links with what they now find. They might have eaten blackberry jam, but this is the first time they have been face-to-face with a blackberry before it is turned into jam.

Much of the discussion is also along the lines of, 'Give me that one. I need it. Put it in the basket. The next one is mine.' They co-operate with each other, respecting each other's space as they all pick blackberries from the brambles together. The boy who holds the basket keeps it still while other children drop blackberries into it. They are learning how to relate to each other with sensitivity, courteously and with co-operation.

Planting in the garden

Children are also given opportunities to plant, again using the edges of the garden, away from trampling feet and the nagging of adults to keep off flowerbeds. Children love to use gardening tools and to dig with a purpose.

Nickie uses a trowel, and makes a hole the right size for the plant. He puts the label in the ground, and enjoys wearing his gardening gloves. The adult shows him some plants that have already grown, so that he gets an idea of how the plant he had put into the ground will grow. He is fascinated and gives the conversation his full attention.

Picking blackberries and talking about them

Open spaces to move in

The brambles are round the edges of the garden. They make very good protection from intruders and vandals, and they provide blackberries and an interesting walk round the perimeter finding and picking them.

Children need to be able to run and leap, jump and skip, hop and use carts, wheeled vehicles, and tricycles, and to dance or use a large parachute together in co-operation, by lifting it up and down so that it makes waving patterns that are enjoyed by all involved. Children might use buckets of water, and 'paint' with rollers or large brushes on the tarmac. In this book there are many examples of children being offered such experiences in different settings of all types.

Through this provision staff can help children to make links with different areas of learning. These differ in the different countries of the UK, but they include, emotional, personal, social, expressive and creative, mathematical and physical communication and language, knowledge and understanding of the world, and literacy development. It is important to realize that a real, direct multi-sensory experience can link with areas of learning in different ways.

Cooking

Cooking is not an area of learning. Neither is riding a bike, or painting, which are learning experiences and opportunities. Quite often adults only link an experience with one area of learning. Painting is, for example, often seen in a narrow way as supporting children's creative development. In fact, painting can be scientific, as children transform paint from powder to sludge to dripping and runny, and change the colours.

In the photograph the children at St Francis nursery class cook, with the support of an adult. This experience is on offer every day as one of the choices children can make. This is an everyday feature of Scottish nurseries.

Children begin with an easy recipe, making one chocolate crispy for themselves, for which they learn to count out one spoonful of each ingredient. They gradually move on to make bread rolls, scones, chappatis, birdcake, etc. The children use a recipe book made by the staff, with easy-to-follow pictures and simple words, counting the measurements in spoonfuls.

Just as it is thrilling for children to be engaged in woodwork, so it is a great pleasure to them to cook. They quickly learn to be safe, and again staff make a careful risk assessment. Some recipes, such as the crispy, use heat from a carefully protected night light (see the photograph). This is always supervised by an adult. Other recipes need an oven in an area with a gate, where children only go if accompanied by an adult. Other recipes, such as fruit salad, do not require any form of heat.

Even very young children can become involved in cooking.

Christopher, who is two years old, was interested in the birds visiitng the Family Centre garden, and was keen to feed them with scraps from snack. He was invited to make bird cake, which involved cutting, counting and sharing. We were reminded by him the next morning that the bird cake was waiting in the fridge to be given to the birds. (Tarlton, 2002)

In the Castlebrae nursery schools and classes, there are opportunities for children to bake each day. Children can also help themselves to a drink and healthy snack during the session, providing it is not too near the lunchtime.

Healthy snacks

Children are taught to put the name tag in their cup into a box, so that staff can see who has had a snack, and to pour themselves a drink. They learn they can have one biscuit with cheese-spread, or piece of fruit (eg banana) or vegetable (eg carrot stick). They are taught to wash up afterwards, and leave the cup and plate to drain dry.

Daily baking opportunities

This tradition comes from the emphasis on what Brehony (2000: 186) describes as a turn-of-the-century Froebelian focus on the 'family in the role of community regenerator'.

Children learn to bake in the St Francis nursery class. They measure out ingredients, stored on shelves accessible to children, counting in spoonfuls with metal spoons. They begin to use more spoonfuls and weights and scales as they become experienced cooks. Each child has his or her own mixing bowl and wooden spoon for stirring and mixing ingredients. The adult helps each child to use a simple recipe book, made by staff, based on Scottish traditions of baking (Foley, 2000).

Each page has a photograph or drawing with a simple line of text.

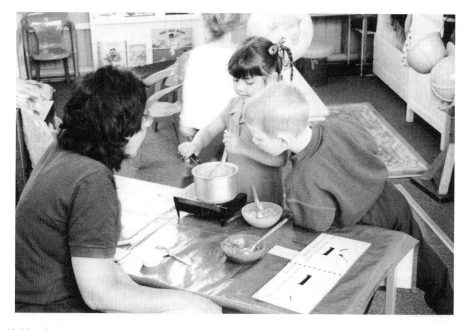

Children learn to cook using a recipe book

The cover, photograph and name of recipe, How to make scones

Page 1   Wash your hands.

Page 2   Put on an apron.

Page 3   You will need: (pictures of utensils with names next to pictures)

Page 4   You will need: (pictures of ingredients)

Page 5   Put 4 tablespoons of flour in your bowl. (pictures and labels)

Page 6   Put 2 tablespoons of margarine in your bowl. (ditto)

Page 7   Rub the margarine with your fingers. (photograph)

Page 8   Break one egg into the bowl. (photograph)

Page 9   Add a little milk. (photograph)

Page 10 Roll the mixture with your hands. (photograph)

Page 11 Roll the mixture out until it is 2 centimetres thick.

Page 12 Cut the scones out with the cutter. (photograph)

Page 13 Put them on a baking tray. (photograph)

Page 14 Cook them in the oven for about 10 minutes. (photograph)

Page 15 Wash up and dry everything. Put it all away. (photograph)

Cooking and all areas of learning

All areas of learning can be addressed through cookery experiences. Those listed areas below reflect all those found in the four UK curriculum frameworks.

Personal, social and emotional development

Cookery develops the personal and emotional aspects of learning. For example, patience is required. It is interesting, and it is a pleasure to eat. It is social. There is talking as you do, passing utensils to each other, washing up together and a general need for co-operation.

Mathematical development

It is very mathematical. There is a procedure with a set sequence to be followed: preparing with hand-washing, gathering everything needed, going through the recipe book in the right order, step by step, weighing out and counting spoonfuls, taking to the oven, sharing the food out, and washing up.

Knowledge and understanding of the world: science, culture and heritage

Science

Cooking helps children to look at the way the ingredients change and undergo chemical reactions as they transform. An egg does not look the same when mixed with butter and flour and then subjected to heat in the oven.

Culture and heritage

Different cultures make food in different ways. Bread is a good example.

At Cameron House the children cooked Scottish traditional food, such as clootie dumpling, shortbread, soup, sair heidies, haggis, tatties and neeps. They made a haggis and at a traditional Burns Supper in January they were involved in the ceremony of piping in the haggis.

Creative, aesthetic and expressive development

Cookery can be creative and children can express themselves through their choices, for instance of the shape of the biscuit, or the decoration of a pie.

Physical, literacy and movement

Cookery is physical, very physical. It helps children to become co-ordinated as they stir and cut, mix and hold bowls and spoons still, or use a rolling-pin. It is also invaluable as a means of encouraging literacy. Children love to 'read' the recipe books and work out the instructions. They love to make cookery books of their favourite recipes, and take them home to try out with family or carers.

None of this learning can take place unless children can use their senses and feedback from movement.

Feeding the senses: the Food for Tot Project

'From the moment we are born, someone is worrying about how or what to feed us.'

This statement is from the resource pack supporting the 'Food for Tot' project based at Greengables Nursery School.

> *It is based around the belief that eating habits developed in early childhood have a significant effect upon adult health. Therefore making positive changes in the diet of young children can prevent the onset of health problems in later life. Recent research suggests a worrying increase in diseases such as obesity and diabetes. These and other so-called 'Illnesses of Civilisation', previously affecting adults, are now occurring in childhood.*
>
> *These factors, coupled with requests for diet-related help and advice from parents attending the cookery group at Greengables, led to the development of 'Food for Tot'* (McKechnie and Jessop, 2002: 5).

Local health visitors working with community dental educators

Jessop works with local health visitors and community dental educators, who all contribute to the Food for Tot project. The courses aim to:

- encourage a balanced diet;
- develop parents' basic dietary knowledge so that they can make positive choices for their families;
- address questions parents may have associated with the diet, health and well-being of their children;
- increase parental confidence and encourage family cohesion;
- develop skills and knowledge that encourage a positive start in young children's lives.

The balance of good health

Group members choosing

The sessions are designed to the group's requests, and can focus on any of the following key issues.

- Diet during pregnancy
- Breast feeding or bottle feeding
- Weaning
- Toddlers
- Family meal times
- Nutrition for the family
- Dental health
- Practical skills (including adults and children cooking together)

The group members decide if they want discussion, taster sessions, practical cookery sessions or videos. They include women who are thinking of having a baby, women who are pregnant, new parents, parents of older babies or toddlers, parents of children under three, and carers of babies and children under three. 'We see this as a positive aspect of this highly successful project which uses a multi-disciplinary approach to work with parents in a community-based setting.' (McKechnie and Jessop, 2002: 15)

Snacks and drinks

A group might look at issues around snacks, and discuss how to give alternatives to sweets and chocolates.

The group might think about drinks. The resource pack helps the group leader to support the discussion, for instance about water. What are the key factors about water? It is:

- cheap;
- freely available;
- needed by our bodies to stay healthy.

It helps:

- replace the water our bodies use or lose;
- our bodies to digest food;
- our bodies to use the nutrients from the food we eat;
- our bodies to stay at the right temperature.

Reduced-fat plain crisps
Savoury biscuits and cheese
Crackers
Breadsticks
Apples

Strawberries
Cheese sticks
Baby-Bel cheeses
Cubes of cheese
Rice cakes
Pitta breads

Oranges/mandarins/ satsumas/clementines
Bananas
Kiwi fruits
Grapes
Nectarines/peaches

Scotch pancakes
Scones
Plain popcorn
Raw carrot sticks
Raw pea pods
Water (plain and mineral)

Alternatives to sweets and chocolates

Two mothers who attended the Food for Tot projects

Susie

'After bottle-feeding my first child, I decided to try breast-feeding my second. After the third day of feeding I thought about stopping and giving him the bottle, as my breasts were really sore. But I kept thinking how much better breast milk was for my child, so I continued to breast-feed him when I got home.

'The difference I noticed with James was that he had a lot of chest infections, stomach upsets and eczema when he was younger. Kyle seems to be a lot healthier.

'The worst thing about breast-feeding was shopping. There were no places available where I could feed him. I tried to express milk when taking him out, but that was hard, and you could try for long enough only to get a small amount of milk. It was fine when I was visiting friends and family as I would use another room. I would never feed in front of anyone else as I never felt comfortable.'

Lindsey

'First thing about breast-feeding is: don't give up too quick and don't listen to horror stories. Yes it doesn't work for everyone, but you'll never know if you don't try. It can be hard to start with, but once you get the hang of it, it can be great – very satisfying watching the baby growing and knowing you're doing that.

'It's best for baby, and all of the people that I know that breast-feed agreed that it's the quickest and easiest way to get back into shape.

It can also be very handy to get some time on your own with the new baby when lots of family and friends are visiting – no need to feel like you're rude, but you need to go and feed the baby.

'It can work just as good on the husband – get him helping with other things about the house, you need to sit down and feed the baby, so you can put your feet up.'

Local outings

A group of children in the nursery class at Peffermill (Castleview) Primary School have visited a local building site. When children are able to engage in active learning by doing real things, they often continue to dwell on what they have experienced afterwards. This is powerful learning.

Paul talking about his digger and using a book to find out how it works

Paul wanted to make a drawing of the machinery that had fascinated him at the building site. He could not name the machine, but with the support of adults who offered him new words, his vocabulary now includes the term 'machinery'. The teacher, Elizabeth Sharp, noted: 'Paul loves the local building site and its machines. He showed such an interest when the class visited the site and he has recreated the visit through his play many, many times over.'

Paul loves the local building site and its machines. He has drawn this.

Bedding down the memory of the real visit

Using non-fiction books

Paul actively seeks out the book about the digger, which is part of the display and interest table made by the staff to help the children reflect on their visit to the building site. He loves to talk about the digger, which is another word he added to his vocabulary.

He uses the book to find out about how the machine works. He makes a construction from the mobilo, and hooks it over the side of an empty paint trolley. He asks, 'Could I build my own house?' And 'What happens if I pump some cement in here?'

Using wooden blocks

He makes a tall building using the hollow block, and places one on the top, which he can look through. He pretends this is his camera. Using the hollow blocks again, he sits behind them, and says he is parking his car. He is wearing his builder's hat.

No substitute for real experience

The importance of direct experience and the way it makes possible the development of real learning cannot be over-emphasized. Experiences such as visiting the building site, become embedded into episodic memories in the brain, to be reactivated and used in later learning. Since it takes a year or two for these to bed down, it is very important to keep the pathways open. Play helps this process, as children reactivate the memory.

Creating play scenarios

Because Paul has plenty of opportunity to play with the wooden blocks and mobilo, look at books, and talk with adults and other children about the building site, the development of learning continues. Learning through the direct experience of his senses and movements has made a firm base through which to develop his learning into pretend play, and to further his understanding of what causes what to work in what way in machinery, and to what effect.

This is developing learning in a broad and deep way:

- through the senses and movement;

- through symbolic behaviour (pretend, imaginative play, drawing, etc);
- through teasing out the cause and effect relationships.

Active learning wherever you go, indoors and outdoors

In this chapter we have discussed active learning both indoors and outdoors. The real, direct experiences we introduce children to influence the learning so that it deepens and develops into more abstract, sophisticated forms over time. Rich learning cannot be rushed. Developing learning means that through the senses and movement children build their understanding of time, space and the reasons for things. Without such experiences children cannot make sense, and unless they actively make sense, they do not learn.

This is so for all children, but it is particularly so for children with complex needs. We have seen how Nielsen (1992) gives first-hand sensory experiences to children with physical and complex needs. Using light poles and boards, she made a 'Little Room' (see pages 38–9) that is just right for an individual child. One child might be encouraged to reach out for bells hanging from the pole above their head; another might reach and bang the sides, or touch a swinging object.

Making sense of learning through the senses

Most children learn through their senses naturally. As babies, they may have been placed in a cot or pram that is like the 'Little Room'.

It is not enough solely to provide clay, sand, water, paint, glue and junk materials, mark-making opportunities, wooden blocks, construction kits, home corners, puzzles, climbing, open space, gardening, book corner, computer, dough, cookery, sewing, woodwork, interactive interest tables and displays, jigsaws, small world, dressing up, and so on.

Using the senses and movement feedback does not automatically lead to higher levels of learning. Developing learning depends on the sense children make of the senses they use. Their learning, quite literally, must 'make sense'.

Adults can help nature along by providing rich experiences which involve children in making sense of the way they use the senses and movement. Then children develop their intellectual lives in an atmosphere which engages their feelings, through interests, and being listened to and talked with. These are extended to deeper learning through symbolic behaviours.

They begin to understand spatial and temporal relationships and the reason why things happen and people behave as they do. This develops all aspects of learning about ideas, feelings and relationships.

In practice

- Do you feel you don't have enough space to provide paint, clay, sand, water, wooden blockplay, woodwork, sewing, home corner, small world, book corner, graphics area and workshop, puzzles, snack bar, cookery, computer, etc, every day? If so, take out as many tables, chairs and closed cupboards as possible.
- Give each child a box next to their peg, instead of a table and chair.
- Do you have open access to the outside for as much of the day as possible? If you are worried that children might not be learning outside, it means your provision is poor.
- Do you add to the basic areas of provision through double provision, such as basic paint-mixing every day, with special techniques on a different table when it seems appropriate? In this way, you can extend the provision as needed in different areas, indoors and outdoors.

Further reading

Bilton, H. (1998) *Outdoor Play in the Early Years: Management and Innovation*. London: David Fulton.

Edgington, M. (2002) *The Great Outdoors: Developing Children's Learning through Outdoor Learning Experiences*. London: Early Education.

Gura, P. (1996) *Resources for Early Learning: Children, Adults and Stuff*. London: Paul Chapman Publishing.

Harding, S. (2001) 'What's Happening with the Bikes?' *Early Childhood Practice: The Journal for Multi-Professional Partnerships* 3(2): 24–42.

Ouvry, M. (2000) *Exercising Muscles and Minds*. London: National Early Years Network.

Ratey, J. (2001) *A User's Guide to the Brain*. London: Little, Brown.

Video: 'Outdoor Play' (Auckland College of Education, Hilary Commission, Auckland Kindergarten Association, ASB Charitable Trust). Available from Private Bag, Symonds St, Auckland, New Zealand.

8

Why is play important?

Key themes

Play is an umbrella word (Bruce, 1991) which is impossible to pin down. It has fascinated thinkers since ancient times, as they observed young children at play. It was Froebel who first embraced the learning that children engage in through their play and made it part of a child's education.

Some theories emphasize the ideas and thoughts children have as they develop their learning through play. Others focus on the way that play helps children to experiment and cope with their feelings, and to deal with them through its self-healing powers. These theories also give us insights into the way play helps children to understand other people and to relate to others. We should not underestimate the way that play also helps children to be physically co-ordinated, which links with the development of their self-esteem and well-being. Free-flow play applies throughout life.

Practitioners are finding practical ways of supporting and extending children's development and learning through play. Different theories offer support in different ways.

A great deal of lip-service is paid to the importance of play in developing the learning of young children. There is widespread confusion about what it is. We need to try to clarify the concept of play, so that we can work effectively with children and their families.

In everyday conversation, it is generally unfair and provoking to ask for precise definitions of familiar words. But when a familiar concept like aggression, intelligence, or personality becomes an object of study, then it must be defined or delineated, at least clearly enough so that those who contribute to the study and those who may benefit from it know they are talking about the same thing. Play has been a particularly recalcitrant notion. (Garvey, 1977: 10)

Play is probably one of the least understood aspects of an early-childhood practitioner's work. In this chapter we will explore the key issues of this complex and sophisticated concept, and look at the contribution play makes in developing learning, in which play is a central mechanism and needs to be nurtured during childhood. This is a challenge for practitioners of all kinds, and for parents too.

Research (Siraj-Blatchford et al., 2002: 115) shows that the richest play is found especially in nursery schools and early-excellence centres, many of which were originally nursery schools, where heads and teachers have trained to a high level in the early years and have a deep understanding of child development and how learning develops in young children. The studies found that play is often thought by practitioners only to involve 'imaginative play'. 'This narrow conceptualisation of play is shared by many other early childhood practitioners for whom play is considered essential, as an activity promoting learning and yet only relevant to some areas of the curriculum. According to Wood and Attfield (1996), despite constant validation from academics (Bruce, 1991; Moyles, 1989) play continues to have an insecure place in delivering the curriculum.' (Siraj-Blatchford et al., 2002: 115)

Pioneers of play

Plato, c. 428–347 BCE

Plato wanted to help children participate in what he called high culture as a means of protecting them from the advance of 'uncivilised influences' (Egan, 1997: 12).

Ideas important to the culture: the forms of knowledge

Plato believed that the human mind has in it an intuitive understanding of the important ideas of the culture. He called these the highest 'forms of knowledge'. He suggested that the important ideas of the culture (the forms of knowledge) are unchanging in an ever-changing world. Education is about the pursuit of these highest forms of knowledge, which are central to the culture.

Play as making the forms of knowledge accessible to young children

Some educators still adhere to the Platonic pursuit of high culture which makes schools separate places of learning from real life. However, most educators of young children, supported by research evidence (Siraj-Blatchford et al., 2002,) now think that play is an important means by which children are helped to connect with high culture.

For example, by creating play scenarios with 'goodies' and 'baddies' (Holland, 2003) children are led to the fundamental aspects of Greek or Shakespearean literature and drama, with time-honoured battles between good and evil. This play benefits from being supported and extended by sensitive adults.

Immanuel Kant, 1724–1804

Immanuel Kant probably has the most holistic approach since Plato (Magee, 1987: 187).

Concepts, our windows on the world

Kant believed that we have windows on the world which are our concepts. Each individual has different experiences, using the senses and feedback from movement, and this has a deep effect on the way we look through the windows which are our concepts. Kant believed that these shared concepts (ideas) lead us to share, dialogue and exchange thoughts, feelings and relationships with each other. They have a unifying effect. According to Collinson (1988: 90), Kant argued 'that knowledge is founded on subjective experiences which are produced by external entities that affect our senses … In this way a subjective sensory experience may be transformed into objective conceptual knowledge.'

Kant's influence on Froebel

Although Kant does not write about play, his thinking influenced the pioneer educator Friedrich Froebel, whose view was that play was an important way in which children organize their learning into a whole.

Friedrich Froebel, 1782–1852

Before theories about play were established (when the discipline of psychology emerged), support for the importance of play came from philosophy for practitioners. Froebel's ideas about play in his schools and learning communities were greatly influenced by Kant, whom he studied while reading mathematics at university.

Play as developing learning

Throughout the history of early childhood practice during the last 100 years, a concept has been handed down from generation to generation of practitioners which presents play as central in the learning of young children.

Friedrich Froebel pioneered the view that play acts as an organizing function which integrates learning and helps children to apply their knowledge and understanding in relation to their developing ideas, feelings, physical bodies and relationships. He was working before there were any theories about play in the modern sense.

Learning developing into a co-ordinated whole through play

Froebel developed a theory drawing on the philosophy of his day. He proposed that play is the way children integrate and bring together what they know, understand and feel into a whole. Play, he believed, shows children applying what they can do and understand at the highest levels of which they are capable. Play makes it possible for very young children to think flexibly, to adapt what they know, try out different possibilities and reach abstract levels of functioning in a way that is appropriate.

Froebel and Vygotsky

The work of Vygotsky resonates with some aspects of Froebel's earlier claims, although he did not know about his work. Froebel argued that play is the highest level of learning and that it is therefore the most spiritual activity of the child. By this he meant that children begin to understand themselves, others and the universe, and play is the organizing mechanism through which this occurs.

Theories such as these outlining the importance of play have only emerged in the last 100 years. But theories do not give us evidence; they give us frameworks through which we can make sense of human behaviour and development and be enabled to make predictions.

Theories help us to explore and gather evidence about the value of play in developing learning.

Theories about play

In this section we look at some of the theories which emerged after Froebel's death, each of which suggests why play is central to the learning of young children.

Work and play have been separated and placed in opposition in several influential early theories of play. The damaging impact of this polarization still lurks today, although in the 1930s Susan Isaacs made an attempt to rescue the situation by suggesting that play is in fact a child's work, which has an air of damage limitation about it. The following two theories divide work from play.

Play as recreation

Play takes huge energy and concentration. It is anything but recreation or relaxation. When the children have wallowed in rich free-flow play, they are exhausted once it fades, and they may then need recreation and the opportunity to relax. This view of play gives it a low status.

Play as the means by which children burn off excess energy

This is another damaging theory about play, one that was influenced by the particular events of its historic and cultural context. This was Herbert Spencer's (1882–1903) theory, which came into being during the industrial revolution at around the time when compulsory schooling was introduced by the Education Act (1872).

The theory is that children are like industrial machines and need to release excess energy and let off steam in the playground between lessons. Children were regarded as cogs in the machinery, like those who worked in the factories. Rough-and-tumble play and play involving lively chasing, were viewed as low-level releases of unwanted energy. Play was necessary to avoid explosions of bottled-up energy.

School playgrounds are still too often influenced by this theory. However, nursery schools never subscribed to it, and the outdoor area was and is regarded as an important half of the learning area. Nursery schools drew on theories about play developing learning at home and in group settings (Brehony, 2000), and did not divide work from play but integrated the two.

Other theories

During the 1920s the new discipline of psychology emerged, and new unpublished theories of play were formed. Stanley Hall (1884–1924) suggested that during play children work through the history of humanity. They are hunters and gatherers, warriors, builders of settlements, farmers, tool-makers, carers of their young, crafts-makers, nomads, law-makers, punishers, justice-makers. They show the development of the species in the correct order. Egan (1997: 27) suggests that he was influenced by Spencer, whom he quotes. 'If there be an order in which the human race has mastered its various kinds of knowledge, there will arise in every child an aptitude to acquire these minds of the same order.' (Spencer, 1861: 76)

By the 1930s more sophisticated theories of play had emerged. This had a huge impact on the way practitioners worked with children in group settings.

Play as preparation for and rehearsal of the future

Karl Groos

In the 1920s Groos developed his theory that children quite naturally prepare for their adult lives by rehearsing adult events and ways of doing things in their play both physically and socially.

Johan Huizinga

Huizinga (1949) went further than this. He argued that civilizations are marked by the phenomenon that adults continue their play into adulthood, the theory of *homo ludens*. This keeps their wits sharpened and their bodies fully functioning, and enables them to be flexible and forward-looking adaptive people.

Jerome Bruner

Bruner (1983: 43) sees play as 'preparation for the technical and social life that constitutes human culture'. During the 1960s Bruner's theory exerted a wide influence. He suggested that mammals have long childhoods because there is so much for them to learn in preparation for adult life. He was uneasy about free-flow play, emphasizing instead games with rules, such as songs, rhymes and peekaboo.

This approach has led to adults dominating the play of children, with methods variously called guided play, structured play, play tutoring or learning the play way. The emphasis is on what Egan (1997: 11) calls the 'homogenisation' of children. The way that play is encouraged in early childhood settings is inevitably affected by the fact that at the heart of schooling is the desire to socialize by homogenizing and inducing conformity. Egan (1997: 12) points out that when pushed to extremes, this can become totalitarian in its demands for conformity.

Adult-dominated tasks are not play

Unfortunately play in group settings, especially in primary schools, too often results in desultory sessions in which children are guided in their play into pre-structured adult-led outcomes. This is not play. It is children being initiated into adult-led tasks, which certainly have their place, and are an important part of direct teaching. However, teaching children to use the tools of a woodwork bench, to cook, to mix paint, showing them how to study beetles without squashing them, reading to them or scribing for them are not play. But all of these things are important for children to learn about.

Play as a process with no product

Play 'free flows' (Bruce, 1991) along, bringing clarification and illumination of ideas, feelings, relationships and understandings of the human body in an entirely different way.

There is a real difference between inculcating children into the culture of adults and encouraging them through their play culture to make sense of the adult world. Kalliala (2002: 32) gives the example of Tommi, who is required to write a composition, but is regularly disappointed because his teacher is not pleased with his efforts at writing. Because he always writes about rally racing, the teacher bans the topic for him. But Mika makes play scenarios about world championship ice-hockey. He makes a rink out of a mat, and has a torch for the spotlight, sings the music and announces the players (ice-hockey cards) as they enter.

In these examples, Tommi is being inculcated into the adult culture, whereas Mika, through his play, is making sense of adult culture.

Pleasure play

This theory of play saw the joy of physical movement as the heart of play. It was pioneered by Charlotte Buhler in the 1930s. It resonates with the health and beauty movement and the outdoor camps for children in woodlands during the summer months in Europe and the US. It emphasizes the pleasure in movement which activates unconscious physical and mental learning. Play is seen as a process with no purpose on the part of the child. This is play aiding natural learning.

Theories about feelings and play

Another unfortunate divide developed with the emergence of psychological theories about human development, which stressed the importance of feelings. Piaget's work was mainly concerned with thoughts and ideas children have, and he had (Piaget, 1952) great respect for the pioneering work of Sigmund Freud on the emotions. His own work did not make a separation of emotion and intellect, which he thought gave different emphases to the various aspects of human development.

> *There is never a purely intellectual action, and numerous emotions, interests, values, impressions of harmony, etc., intervene for example, in the solving of a mathematical problem. Likewise, there is never a purely affective act, e.g., love presupposes comprehension. Always and everywhere, in object-related behaviour as well as in interpersonal behaviour, both elements are involved because the one presupposes the other. There are those who are more interested in people than things or abstractions and vice versa, which makes the former appear more sentimental and the latter more arid, but it is merely a question of different behaviour and different emotions. Each necessarily employs both intelligence and affectivity.* (Piaget, 1964: 34)

Both the psychodynamic theories arising from Freud's work and Piagetian theory made the concept of balance central. Freud saw this as a fixed state (homeostasis), whereas for Piaget balancing (equilibration) was more like riding a bicycle. The importance of play is that it keeps children well balanced in both theories.

Anna Freud, 1895–1982

Interestingly, Anna Freud, who was an outstanding teacher as well as an analyst (Coles, 1992), was criticized by her colleague Melanie Klein (Kohan, 1986: 38–40; Bell, 1999: 11) because Freud saw that children are whole people first, and that even children who have experienced trauma benefit from as natural a childhood as possible, surrounded by love, nurtured, encouraged and helped to play.

> *Anna Freud's preference for respectful observation rather than intrusive assault in clinical exploration as well as selection of candidates is reflected in her well known struggles with Melanie Klein … who was very much a follower of the early [Sigmund] Freud who explored the unconscious with daring and courageous conjecture. She believed the child analyst can know a lot about the preverbal child, and can work with conviction and dispatch to obtain an analytic intimacy with young children not unlike the kind that develops between analysts and their grown-up patients … Miss Freud was inclined to be wary of what she regarded at best as the surmises and guesses of those who followed Mrs. Klein.* (Coles, 1992: 121)

Play as healing emotional pain and helping children to be forward-looking

Anna Freud believed that play was a cathartic experience for children. In their play children can move in and out of reality. As they play they can exert some control over their lives. They can experiment with how to deal with their feelings so that they can better manage their emotions. As well as the conflicts and sadnesses of life, play also helps children to experience joy and be forward-looking. Play helps children to interpret experiences and makes them become whole people.

Vivian Gussin Paley, whose work resonates in a modern way with the approach of Anna Freud, shows how children play out what frightens them in order to control their fears:

> *'Help, help!' Barney screams. 'I'm destroying! The king! The invisible bad king! He told me to get you. Now I'm all chained up. I'm the glue person!'*
>
> *'Don't worry, Barney bat. I'll save you. Here, I'm melting you with my face. There! Now break yourself out.'*
>
> *'Whew! Thanks, Fredrick. You saved me. I was starting to die. Now I can live for the whole forever.'* (Gussin Paley, 1986: 118)

Melanie Klein, 1882–1960

Melanie Klein, as we saw above, took a different view. She believed that children could be helped through analysis at a very young age. She did not consider it necessary to wait until the oedipal stage (between four and six years of age), which followed the oral (birth to two years) and anal stages (between two and four years). She disagreed with Anna Freud's caution, instead making 'confident and suggestive inquiry' (Coles, 1992: 121), a concept which influenced British psychoanalysis at the time. She dismissed Anna Freud's questions.

- *How is one to do psychoanalytic work with children scarcely able to speak?*
- *How can re-enactment of childhood attitudes toward parents get going in children who are only now beginning to develop their initial, sustained attitudes toward their parents?*
- *How exact is the analogy between children's play with toys, or their drawings, on the one hand, and the 'free associations' that adult analysands [those analysed] are asked to produce, on the other?* (Coles, 1992: 121–2)

Erik Erikson, 1902–1994

Erik Erikson was a student of Anna Freud. He believed that through their play children become partners with their futures. He invited children to construct scenes based on imaginary films, and was interested in the way that the play scenarios they invented seemed to serve as metaphors for their future lives and 'intimately related to the dynamics of the person's life history' (Erikson, 1963: 95). The scenes reflected their interests and fears, their strengths and challenges. He visited the children as adults later and found that their lifestyles held resonances of their childhood play (Erikson, 1963).

Erikson established eight stages of development, each of which involved a dilemma (Maier, 1978: 132; Bruce and Meggitt, 2002). In the first stage, the dilemma is between trust and mistrust. The second stage is that of the play stage, when autonomy emerges (or not). Through play children develop initiative and are strengthened to face disappointments and failures and to approach life with involvement and purpose.

Erikson's view was that children in their free-flow play (Bruce, 1991) deal with their experiences by creating a model situation which they can master, plan and experiment with. He says the child 'relives their past and thus relives left-over affects. He anticipates the future from the point of view of a corrected and shared past' (Erikson, 1963: 222)

Donald Winnicott, 1896–1971

Winnicott developed his understanding of play through what he called the transitional object. This can be a substitute for people who are important for the child emotionally, when they are not present. A transitional object can also help the child to enjoy the presence of those they love. In short, a transitional object links the child to loved people. 'In order to give a space to playing I postulated a *potential space* between the mother (carer) and the baby. This potential space varies a very great deal according to the life experiences of the baby in relation to the mother or mother-figure, and I contrast this potential space (a) with the inner world ... and (b) with actual, or external reality.' (Winnicott, 1971: 47–8)

Transitional objects and play

Transitional objects work in two ways. As well as being a natural and healthy link with those they love, they also support the child in early imaginative play. The teddy stands for the absent father who will return after work, but also has a life of imaginative play with the child, taking meals together, sleeping together and having adventures together.

> Jason, a summer-born child, started school in a very formal reception class in which the teacher introduced the formal group teaching of literacy and number work for two hours a day from the autumn entry term. After a week he began to cry and say he did not want to go to school. He said he found the work too hard. His mother spoke to the classteacher, who unwillingly agreed that he could bring his teddy to school with him. After the first day when teddy joined him, his mother asked him if he had found school better. He said he did, because when he had tears in his eyes he could wipe them with teddy's ears, and teddy would whisper, 'Never mind, you will soon be at home.'
>
> He had found comfort from his transitional object when separated from his home, linking him to the comfort of his mother. He had also taken teddy into imaginative play which eased his unhappiness. Play is about dealing with difficulties and sadness as much as with happiness. He was being asked to behave in ways which were too formal too soon, and without the teddy might have coped less well in a far from ideal situation.

Objects of transition

These are different from transitional objects; they do not take on an imaginative life, or stand for someone in their absence, or increase enjoyment in someone they love's company. Not all children have transitional objects, or imaginative friends. Objects of transition (Bruce, 2001b: 77) are different because they simply ease the transition from home to the group or childminder and then back to the home.

Winnicott, like Erikson, was more inclined to the views of Anna Freud than of Melanie Klein.

Cognitive theories of play

The theories that deal with feelings are different from the other theories in this chapter, because they make strong links between childhood play and adult creativity, that is, how childhood's imaginative, pretend play develops into drama, dance or music improvisations, artistic happenings or scientific problem-solving and hypothesizing.

These theories, which focus on how children develop their ideas and thoughts, see play as part of childhood only, possibly implying that play turns into the ability to take part in games with rules during middle childhood.

Jean Piaget, 1896–1980

Play as unifying learning

Although Piaget (1951) stresses the way early childhood play turns into games with rules, he agrees with Anna Freud, Klein, Erikson and Winnicott that childhood play unifies ideas, feelings and relationships and the physical body movements.

Play as giving balance to learning

Piaget agreed that the psycho-dynamic theories of play that balance (equilibrium) is of central importance, and that play contributes to children being well-balanced. According to him, we can never reach a constant state of balance. It is a state of becoming rather than being. Free-flow play is a process, and not a steady state. He called the process of balancing equilibration, which has two aspects, accommodation and assimilation. Accommodation is about adapting to situations, and assimilation is about adding the familiar to what is known already. Play is mainly to do with assimilation. It is about applying what has already been learnt.

Three kinds of play

Piaget thought there were three kinds of play, which developed in order.

- First there was sensory-motor play, which involved the senses and movement. This is the play of babies and toddlers.
- Then there was pretend, imaginative play during early childhood.
- Finally, there were games with rules, which led into sports and rule-bound games in middle childhood. This kind of play was with objects and also with people.

From early childhood play to games with rules

Piaget saw a linear development from play to games with rules, rather than understanding free-flow play as something that develops into drama, literature, dance choreography, musical composition, creative writing, painting, research in science or experimentation with mathematically elegant answers during middle childhood, adolescence and adult life. He did think of games and play as two different aspects of a network of learning which feed off and into each other.

The high status of play in developing learning in young children

Piaget's theories have had a major impact on early childhood education since the 1960s, because they stress the central importance of play as a learning mechanism during early childhood (although he thought it faded by the end of middle childhood).

Lev Vygotsky, 1896–1934

Learning through social relationships

Since the 1990s Vygotsky's theory of play has not been explored as much as his view that children participate in their culture and learn what is important for them to know through social relationships with others, especially adults.

Play as creating a zone of potential learning

Vygotsky sees play as creating a zone of potential development, in which children operate at their highest level of functioning, beyond their present-day possibilities, so that they become ahead of themselves. Both adults or more skilled children can be catalysts in this process. Vygotsky (1978: 101) considers play to be 'a leading factor in development'. This makes it 'the highest level of preschool development. The child moves forward essentially through play activity.' (Vygotsky, 1978: 102–3)

Emphasis on imaginative play

In Vygotsky's theory play is conceived of as imaginative play. 'Thus, in establishing criteria for distinguishing a child's play from other forms of activity, we conclude that in play a child creates an imaginary situation.' (Vygotsky, 1978: 95)

Because he has a narrow view of what play is, he states: 'Play in an imaginary situation is essentially impossible for a child under three in that it is a novel form of behaviour liberating the child from constraints.' (Vygotsky, 1978: 96)

Play for Vygotsky is the way that children free themselves from the constraints of reality. 'The child sees one thing but acts differently in relation to what he sees. Thus, a condition is reached in which the child begins to act independently of what he sees.' He adds, that 'it is terribly difficult for a child to sever thought (the meaning of a word) from object.' (Vygotsky, 1978: 97)

Emphasis on language in play

Because young children do not find it easy to separate the meanings of words from what they represent, the development of imaginative play is linked with language development.

Play becoming games with rules

Vygotsky agrees with Piaget that imaginative play leads into games with rules. 'Just as the imaginary situation has to contain rules of behaviour, so every game with rules contains an imaginary situation.' (Vygotsky, 1978: 95) He also agrees that childhood play turns into sports and games with rules in middle childhood. However, Piaget has a broader view of play, more in tune with modern research on the early development of the brain, which suggests that play involves the senses and movement as well as developing the imagination and rule behaviour.

Other theorists of play we have looked at in this chapter believe that play is possible from birth to death, and not, as Vygotsky suggests, mainly from three years old until middle childhood. This is because play is not just imaginative, although that is an important feature (Moyles, 1989; Bruce, 1991, 2001a; Wood and Attfield, 1996; Siraj-Blatchford et al, 2002).

Vygotsky stresses the social side of play more than Piaget. They both see people and objects as important in play. Unlike Piaget's or Froebel's theories, or the affective theories of play, Vygotsky puts the emphasis on social relationships, imaginative play and language. This is a narrow view of play compared with other theories, which means that it is of limited use when working with babies and toddlers, children with disabilities and children who have suffered trauma.

Attempting to define play and pin it down

It is clear from the literature that although play has been discussed for centuries, there is no clear definition of it. It is still an umbrella word (Garvey, 1977; Bruce, 1991). This has made it a very hazy concept.

A trawl through the research literature on play (in the English language) reveals some recurring themes which build a picture for us of the contribution play makes to developing learning. Translations from other languages, especially those from the Nordic languages, suggest that whereas in the US and UK adults are seen to have a leading role in playing with children, in other parts of the world, including mainland Europe, children's play culture is respected and adults do not dominate so much (Kalliala, 2004, in press). Lofdahl's study of hegemonies (power relationships) in children's play culture shows how children are active agents in their own learning.

As children play, resistance to power relationships appears, and children use their agency and become powerful meaning makers as they develop their knowledge. Together, children show their knowledge of daily life with its winners and losers, decision makers, norms and rules to be followed. Play gives opportunities to try out what is not allowed, to test boundaries and be aware of what can happen if they are broken. Rather than seeing, in children's actions and play, fear of authority, children show what they know about, how to deal with authorities, and how to gain authority. (Lofdahl, 2002: 45)

Play – does it develop outside in or inside out?

In Chapter 1 we looked at the way brain development is triggered by the environment as children learn through and from other people. We saw how these social experiences quite literally sculpt the brain (Meade, 2003). We are individuals. Froebel in the nineteenth century believed that it is the role of the educator to make the inner outer and the outer inner (Liebschner, 1991, 1992). But which comes first?

On the one hand, no one can play unless the mechanisms for play are formed in the human brain (the inner). On the other, play will not develop unless the external environment triggers the mechanisms causing play to develop (the outer). Teasing out which comes first is at the centre of all the theories of play we have looked at in this chapter. Both the development of the inner life (through the brain) and the outer life (through the people we meet and the experiences we have) influence the way play is supported and extended by adults. This in turn has an impact on the way the brain develops (Brown, 1998).

Looking for clues in the natural play of children at home

Dunn (1995) looks at natural play in the family setting at home. She found that toddlers engaged in pretend play with their older brothers and sisters as part of everyday life. The older children would give specific instructions on how to role-play, and guide them into the narrative of the play. This helped the toddlers to participate appropriately.

Dunn's belief in the importance of studying children's play in natural everyday settings at home makes a stark contrast with the kind of play found in many group early-childhood settings. This may be because in these situations adults feel the need to teach play, but they tend to do so in a very different way from the way older siblings teach their younger brothers and sisters to play.

Play in early childhood groups: Vivian Gussin Paley

Gussin Paley writes about children playing in early years settings or schools. One of the problems practitioners face in emphasizing the importance of play in these group settings is that they may feel pressured to teach play directly rather than causing it to arise through indirect teaching.

Gussin Paley avoids over-teaching. Her strength lies in the way she describes play in fine detail as it unfurls, so that we share the atmosphere she creates in which play can thrive. This is planning an environment conducive for play, complementary in spirit to the documents guiding the play curricula of the four UK countries, the Steinerian approach articulated by Jenkinson (2002), the theories of Anna Freud or the focus on children's play culture prevalent in the literature of other Euopean countries (Kalliala, 2003). It is planned play because the adults set up atmospheres and provide time, spaces and their informed support in encouraging children to play (Singer and Singer, 1990).

In her books, (1984, 1986, 1990) Gussin Paley like Jerome and Dorothy Singer (1990) emphasizes the importance of providing children with places to play, play materials and adult support, but not adult domination of the play. She extends play by offering to scribe stories children want to tell her, which have arisen as they play. She helps them to realize implicitly that these play scenarios can be written down as literature.

Gussin Paley extends children's play into the canon of drama and literature of their culture, with some dance and music here and there. She does not write about the way she extends play into two- or three-dimensional art, or into mathematical explorations or scientific hypothesizing and experimentation. Her work has a fine focus within the range she has chosen. She leads children from the inner to the outer, linking them with their culture, with literature and drama in particular.

Janet Moyles

Moyles (1989) has developed a play spiral in which the inner and the outer are addressed in succession. After a period of free exploration of materials, the practitioner directs the play. 'Appropriately directed play will ensure the child learns from his or her current state of knowledge and skill' (Moyles, 1989: 17). She then, after the period of directed play, encourages children to initiate their own free play using what they have been taught in the directed and guided play. Adults withdraw and encourage children to develop their own play. The adult does not participate in the children's free play, but rather observes it and then teaches, acting on the observations.

Where does this lead us?

Neither Gussin Paley nor Moyles participates and joins in with the children's free play. Both, from their different perspectives, see free play as independent of adults. Moyles sees free play as the part of her spiral where children need to be left alone to try out what they have learnt through the adult directed play. Gussin Paley believes that she does not know the rhythms and cadences of the play sufficiently to be able to do this.

> *Christopher does not try to enter the ongoing play, now that he realises it is play, but his syncopation is off. I would gladly teach him the method, if I could, but my rhythms don't work either. He must watch the children, find his own style, and practice a great deal. One thing I can do for Christopher is to stop jumping in so quickly. By substituting my own cadence too often, I may be delaying his adaptation to the rhythm of the group.* (Gussin Paley, 1986: 84)

Her way of taking the inner play of children and connecting it with curriculum content is to have discussions around but not during the play, especially when scribing the stories of children, or at group time.

It is somewhat of a chicken-and-egg situation to determine whether the outer should come before the inner in developing children's play, but we can see that the starting-point will make a big difference to the way adults develop learning through play.

Wood (1990) unlike Moyles and Gussin Paley, focuses on the outer aspects of play. She gives a major role to the adult and emphasizes the importance of developing links to official curriculum documents. Gussin Paley works with the inner aspects of play, giving backstage and follow-up support. Moyles alternates free play and direct teaching through tutoring. Wood and Moyles write about children from 3 years, and it is only recently that Gussin Paley has begun to write books about younger children (2001).

In practice

- Do you feel that children are learning more when they are doing something tangible? Doing a drawing or painting? Making a wooden block-play construction? Sitting in a group doing something an adult leads?
- If so, perhaps your home corner, workshop area, garden, are not cultivating children's possibilities for free-flow play. Children can only play richly and deeply if they have a conducive environment. They need time to play, places to set up their play and people who help them to play.
- Do you observe children enough to be able to realize when they need help with discussing what to do when two people want to be in the same role?
- Do you observe with enough understanding to work out how to extend the provision to cultivate children developing through their play a storyline, or hopping, skipping and jumping, or playing with patterns of pebbles?
- Do you remind yourself that play helps flexible thinking, that is, different ways of doing the same thing? Supposing, as if, pretending, or three thousand ways to tie a knot?

Further reading

Bruce, T. (1991) *Time to Play in Early Childhood Education*. London: Hodder and Stoughton.

Gussin Paley, V. (1984) *Boys and Girls: Superheroes in the Doll Corner*. Chicago, IL: University of Chicago Press.

Gussin Paley, V. (1986) *Mollie is Three*. Chicago, IL: University of Chicago Press.

Gussin Paley, V. (1990) *The Boy Who Would Be a Helicopter*. Cambridge, MA: University of Harvard Press.

Holland, P. (2003) *We Don't Play with Guns Here: War, Weapon and Superhero Play in the Early Years*. Maidenhead: Open University Press.

Jennings, J. (2002) 'A Broad Vision and a Narrow Focus', *Early Childhood Practice: The Journal for Multi-Professional Partnerships* 4(1): 50–60.

Moyles, J. (1989) *Just Playing? The Role and Status of Play in Early Childhood*. Buckingham: Open University Press.

9

The essentials of play

Key themes

- Research is showing how the brain uses first-hand experience (feature no. 1).
- Our understanding of rule-based behaviour in humans and other animals is developing (feature no. 2).
- Play props (feature no. 3) are being transformed by new technology (Newson and Newson, 1979: 235–8).
- We keep exploring the differences between the learning involved in choosing to play and adult-led learning (feature no. 4).
- Our understanding of pretending and role-play rehearsals for future life is increasing with work on symbol using (features nos. 5 and 6).
- The importance of personal space, as well as companionships and co-operative play, is another area of research which is continuing (features nos. 7 and 8).
- Our understanding of a child's developing possibility to have an interest and personal agenda is growing continually (feature no. 9).
- In this chapter we see young children wallowing and showing us their latest learning as they play (features nos. 10 and 11).
- This learning has a heart. Free-flow play has its own characteristics in action, making a co-ordinated whole (feature no. 12).

The 12 features of free-flow play (Bruce, 1991, 1996, 2001a) emerged from the wealth of literature that exists on play either in English or translated into English. They have at times been called indicators for quality play (Bruce, 1996). They are a mechanism through which to think about play as it flows along. The observations can then be used to inform the planning, support the play and help children to extend their own play. The features apply to any age of child or adult (DFES, 2002), and can be used with children with special educational needs and disability throughout life. The 12 features of free-flow play draw on the areas of solidarity between theories and diverse disciplinaries, and converging evidence available about how to give holistic, consistent and coherent help to practitioners in developing play in ways which respect the depth of involvement children show at play.

When seven or more features are present during play, we are likely to see effective learning.

The 12 features of free-flow play (Adapted from Bruce, 1991)

1. In their play children use the first-hand experiences they have had in life.
2. Play does not conform to pressures to conform to external rules, outcomes, purposes or directions. Because of this, children keep control of their lives in their play.
3. Play is a process. It has no products. When the play ends, it vanishes as quickly as it arrived.
4. Children choose to play. It is intrinsically motivated. It arises when the conditions are conducive, spontaneously, and it is sustained as it flows.
5. Children rehearse the future in their play. Play helps children to learn to function, in advance of what they can do in the present.
6. Play takes children into a world of pretend. They imagine other worlds, creating stories of possible and impossible worlds beyond the here and now in the past, present and future, and it transforms them into different characters.
7. Play can be solitary, and this sort of play is often very deep. Children learn who they are and how to face and deal with their ideas, feelings, relationships and physical bodies.
8. Children and/or adults can play together, in parallel (companionship play), associatively or co-operatively in pairs or groups.
9. Play can be initiated by a child or an adult, but adults need to bear in mind that every player has his or her own personal play agenda (which he/she may be unaware of) and to respect this by not insisting that the adult agenda should dominate the play.
10. Children's free-flow play is characterized by deep concentration, and it is difficult to distract them from their learning. Children at play wallow in their learning.

11.   In play children try out their recent learning, mastery, competencies and skills and consolidate them. They use their technical prowess and confidently apply their learning.

12.   Children at play co-ordinate their ideas and feelings and make sense of relationships with family, friends and culture. Play is an integrating mechanism which allows flexible, adaptive, imaginative, innovative behaviour. Play makes children into whole people, able to keep balancing their lives in a fast changing world.

1 First-hand experience used in play

Play feeds on real experience. It would be unethical to deprive children of normal experience on purpose, but there have been situations (such as in the Romanian orphanages) which demonstrate how lack of real experiences constrains the development of free-flow play with all its features.

A fundamental principle of early-childhood education is to give full opportunities to learn directly through the senses with freedom of movement, both indoors and outdoors. This opens up the potential for rich free-flow play, which depends also on rich experience if it is to bring depth to the development of learning. In high-quality play children in fact use many of the features of play.

Providing spaces and materials for play

In the St Francis Primary School nursery class, the staff make careful provision in the home corner, which is regularly reviewed and developed based on their observations, and is linked with curriculum areas of learning. At the period under discussion it was like this.

Bedroom area resources
Large bed for children/dolls
Small bed for children/dolls
Bunk beds for dolls
Unworkable TV with remote control
Chest-of-drawers for dolls' clothes
Mirror
Dressing-up clothes for children
Four dolls, two male, two female, multicultural
Accessories for babies: bottle, potty, toothbrush, small containers, etc.

Clothes for dolls, prams for dolls and children.

Kitchen area resources
Fridge, cooker, dresser, sink, table and chairs
Iron, ironing-board and clothes-airer
Brush, mop, Hoover with dust-buster, small brush, dustpan and pail
Calendar, diary, telephone, telephone book, note pad, pencil
Books to read to babies, newspapers, magazines, catalogues, restaurant take-away lists and address book
Cups, saucers, cutlery, pots, kettle, cooking utensils and bowls
Scales with weights plus recipe books
Baby's high-chair.

The richer the experiences, the richer free-flow play

These play materials help the children to play using the real experiences they have had in everyday life. The richer the experiences, the richer the free-flow play. In this nursery, writes the teacher, in a display for parents and colleagues visiting the Castlebrae exhibition (2002) of children learning though play:

> *Christina and Stephanie enjoy participating in baking activities, and while the scones were baking in the oven, the girls moved to the playhouse to repeat the activity there. Stephanie 'reads' from the recipe book provided, uses the weights to balance ingredients (small bricks) while Christina prepares the dining area to eat the 'cake' after mixing the ingredients in her bowl.*
> (Lamb, 2002)

The teacher also describes how Brandon pretends to be the baby, with Helen as 'mother' feeding him. Brandon has recently had a baby brother at home.

Physical play

Play is not always pretend play. Much of the play that goes on in childhood is developed from using the senses and movement purely. The children at Children's House Nursery School are using every sense in their physical play. They use touch to hold the bar skilfully. They judge distances between the pole, themselves and their friends. They listen to each other and talk about strategies they are using to develop their play. They are out of doors, and so

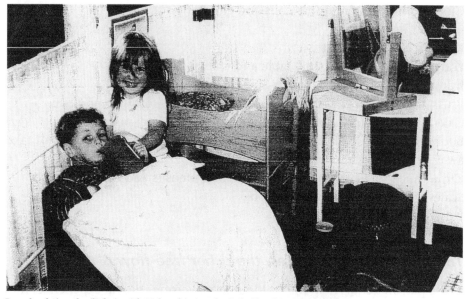

Brandon being the 'baby', with Helen, his 'mother', feeding him

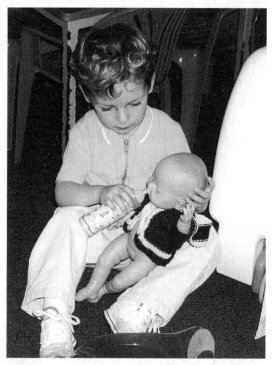

Brandon with baby doll after his baby brother was born

the smells are quite different from indoor play. Background noise is important. Outside it is possible to be noisier without causing the stress and over-excitement that quickly arises in a confined indoor space. They taste the air, which is full of energy-giving oxygen feeding the brain and opening it up to learning. They move with increasing skill, and gain kinaesthetic feedback in doing so.

One boy watches his friends, then tries a gentle swing on to the pole, and moves into a daring upside-down 'hang'. We can trace similar sensual movement play in all of these children.

Physical play

There are links here with theories discussed in Chapter 8: Buhler (pleasure and practice play); Piaget (sensory-motor, cause and effect and symbolic play); Groos (rehearsal play).

2 Making up rules of your own during play

In their free-flow play children take control such that they avoid becoming overwhelmed by life. They can make sense of what is happening and how people behave, and face situations, cope and deal with their futures with more confidence and better well-being. Having a sense of control is a huge factor in developing a sense of balance in life, and becoming a whole person. Children can experiment with rules in their play. They rehearse adult rules, break them and make new ones.

> For example, in the nursery class at St Francis Primary School, Jo is rehearsing rules she has seen people use in relation to knives. She shows us that she has a great deal of knowledge about cutting with knives. Christina and Stephanie have decided the rule is that the small bricks stand for scones.
>
> The children in the photograph, who are involved in physical play on the pole, have made up rules which keep them from getting too close, and lead to pauses which give turns to other swingers.

There are links here with the work of Garvey, Vygotsky and Anna Freud, all of whom emphasize how children gain control of their lives through their play.

3 Making products and play props

Play has no products, but it uses products which are made commercially; created by imaginative children and used in their play, together with found objects and materials.

Play cannot be pinned down

The whole point about play is that it cannot be pinned down. It flows. It is on the move. As it begins to fade away, it vanishes into thin air. If it is too fleeting in its duration, it means that it never got under way with any satisfaction for the players. It needs to be sustained if it is to do any good in developing learning. Children need time to play, spaces to play in and people who are helpful in supporting and extending free-flow play. It will do nothing for their learning if they only have 10 minutes or so to develop their play after finishing their work, since 10 minutes is simply not enough. It takes a bit of time to get into the play, and for its rhythms and conditions to come right, so that the play can be sufficiently deep.

If children know that they do not have enough time to get going in their play, the play may become over-excited and unfocused, or desultory. They do not put in the huge effort that play takes because they can see it is pointless. Jenkinson (2003) is concerned that in day-care setting older children know there is no point in starting a play scenario as they are sure to be interrupted. Children need time to play, which is (why I gave the title 'Time to Play' to the book I wrote on the subject of play in 1991).

Children go beyond needing real play props, especially if they are encouraged to do so, as they are at St Francis School. The cutlery and cooking pots are reality props, but the bricks are only slightly like food. This allows great freedom in deciding what the food will be. Plates of plastic food constrain the imagination.

> *Elaine has set the table and is preparing the meal. The kitchen storage jars contain a variety of small bricks to develop imaginative play regarding food. She has set the cutlery out on the table as she sees it should go. Her cooking pots are 'in use' on the cooker and she is preparing these bricks to be presented as food.* (Lamb, 2002)

Children begin to find their own play props, and to make them. The children at Prestonfield Primary School have visited the sea. They use this first-hand experience in their play scenarios, but are adding props as they need.

Sea play

Practitioners need to develop with the children clear boundaries about what equipment may and may not be raided to turn into a play prop in another area. A box of old oddment wooden blocks might be raided, but not the set of wooden blocks. Children need to understand the limits to what they can do in order that they can be free to be creative in their free-flow play. Adults who admire their efforts in this and discuss decisions with them help the play to flow richly. These are 'shared, sustained conversations' which develop learning (Siraj-Blatchford et al, 2002: 48).

The children at St Francis School used playhouse resources in their free-flow play. They are free to use props they develop because they are secure about what is and is not allowed, and can ask adults if they are unsure.

> *All the red chairs have been gathered by the children from several classroom areas, but the focus has been the old TV set, which is being used as the dash-board of a space ship. This play was instigated by Shaun and Danny.* (Lamb, 2002)

This links with the theories of Piaget and Vygotsky, who both stress how children develop as symbol users in their play, which involves making something stand for something else.

4 Choosing to play

Children cannot be forced to learn. It is no good deciding what children ought to know and then try to make them learn and perform accordingly, because this results in over-teaching. The most effective teaching takes the view that children are biologically driven to be active learners. Another way of putting this is to say that children are intrinsically motivated to learn.

Children whose intrinsic motivation has been damaged from babyhood and from toddler times onwards through being channelled into adult-led learning do not play well. Children who are used to following an adult's lead and can follow adult-set tasks do not learn how to think for themselves, to be flexible thinkers with imagination, creativity and problem-solving skills. They come to see adults as people who show you how to do things, rather than people who open up possibilities for you to do your own thinking.

Intrinsic motivation is protected when children can make good, effective use of what they already know, and are able to use this to access what they do not know, with adults and other children helping them. Gopnik et al. (1999) stress that this is crucial in developing learning in young children. Play, which is intrinsically motivated by nature, has a massive contribution to make in the learning process.

Children are more likely to choose to play if practitioners create an atmosphere which makes them feel safe about entering into play mode and speaking in their first language. Being free to speak deepens the play.

Sadman and Warda enjoy domestic play together, conversing in Bengali. They have taken the dolls from the house corner in one room for a 'drive' in the car in the other room. (Lamb, 2001)

5 Rehearsing and recasting pasts, futures and possibilities

Play lifts children from the here and now. It allows children to create alternatives to the way things are. It opens up possibilities for new ways of doing things, visiting the past, outer space, under the sea, or the future, as well as rearranging the present. Play allows children to function at the highest levels of learning of which they are capable.

It allows children to experiment with life and to imagine, supposing this or that were true. It brings flexibility of thinking, so that ideas, feelings, relationships and physical movement can be explored.

Intellectual development, according to neuroscientists, is about adaptability and flexibility of thought. Calvin (1996) suggests that intelligence is about deciding what to do when you do not know what to do.

Free-flow play helps children to consider and deal with moral dilemmas. The narratives (stories) that develop involve characters with thoughts and feelings, such that children entering into play begin to reflect on how it feels to be a 'baddy', a victim or a 'goody'. They are helped in the development of theory of mind as they play. So other people think as they do? What is it like to be someone else, who may think and feel very differently? It is little wonder that Froebel, who pioneered learning through play in the nineteenth century, believed play is the most spiritual activity of the child, because it helps children to know themselves and others and relate to the universe.

6 A world of pretend

Free-flow play opens up the possibilities for children to pretend. They can pretend that they are other people, and try out the roles of adults they live with or meet in their work situations. This is usually referred to as role play. This allows children to act in advance of their present lives. They can ride cars, keep shops, look after babies, as if they were adults. Play allows children to do these things safely, away from the constraints of real life. This kind of play involves fantasy, because it is within the realms of possibility.

Dressing-up clothes

Children delight in dressing-up clothes. Transformations are at the heart of adult drama, as are the battles between good and evil. Holland points out that what she terms 'war, weapon and superhero play' are often seen as: 'simply dictated by films, videos and TV series, which have limited and repetitive content based crudely on a struggle between good and evil and thus offer children little in terms of extended imaginative play. Moreover, children are re-enacting scenarios where force, often violent, wins out, which contradicts practitioners' efforts to resolve conflict peacefully.' (Holland, 2003: 33)

Good and evil

This is not always how practitioners see such play themes. For those of us who have for many years felt that the struggles between good and evil have a place in play in early-childhood settings, Holland's research helps us to work with consistency, in ways that are well thought through.

> *We have power and must use it wisely. Using our physical power or moral authority to prevent children from hurting themselves or others must be viewed as an acceptable use of that power, but to use our power to colonize their fantasy worlds is surely heading down the road of control and compliance in an altogether different direction. If we subject them to our authority at that level do we not perhaps run the risk of teaching children to resist us, to assert their autonomy at any cost or, alternatively, to comply to whoever holds greatest power sparingly and reflectively, might we not teach children that it is possible to negotiate across difference and that force against force is not the only response to conflict?* (Holland, 2003: 100)

Going into a world of pretend and controlling when you want to leave it

Feature no. 3 shows how children use representations as play props in their play scenarios. In the world of pretend, we see that children create new identities which last for the duration of the play, knowing that they can safely escape back into reality and become themselves again whenever they choose.

This is powerful stuff – almost magic. Wearing the clothes of another helps them in this process. At first they are just a look-alike, but then they learn how to get into the role, helped by others. This will help them towards later creative writing.

> *Kieran loves to dress up, and he pretends he is going to a wedding. He is wearing a veil over his large brimmed hat, a jacket, skirt and a large bag. He also enjoys dressing up and dancing in the music corner. Not long after, Kieran drew a series of pictures, taking for his topic a family wedding, then each picture had its story scribed. This collection of pictures was made into a book with a title, author and illustrator printed. Kieran proudly took his book home to his family for them to read, and of course, he made a valiant attempt to 'read' it for them.* (Lamb, 2002)

During play, children can pretend to be dogs, cats, superheroes and heroines, cartoon characters, fairies, witches, goblins and the like. These characters do not deal with rehearsal for adult life, but they allow experimentation with reality and fantasy. Again costumes and props can ease the process into the imaginary world, but so can movement. Props are not always necessary. Arms outstretched can be a better way of turning into an aeroplane. Fantasy play is not within the realms of possibility; it is not possible for the child to become a dog or a witch.

Children can also pretend that objects are something else. A story-book can become a diary. A pencil can become a spoon. This frees the mind to be flexible and to reach deep levels of thinking and feeling, as well as dizzy heights of imagination.

7 Playing alone

Solitude is not the same as loneliness. There is not enough solitude in the busy pace of modern life. Personal space is important in the development of creativity and the imagination. Many creative and imaginative adults have spent time with themselves as children (Storr,1989). At the heart of creativity is the need to gather ideas and dwell on feelings and relationships and embodiment. These are then incubated, later to emerge, often with a struggle and discomfort on the part of the creator, into something creative. This can be a scientific or mathematical theory, a choreographed dance, or musical composition, or a piece of art, drama or literature. Time to oneself is crucial in the creative process.

Just as solitude is not the same as being lonely, so it does not automatically mean that a child is left unsupported in learning without any help. There has been a problem during recent years, became the emphasis has been on the major role of the adult in actively teaching children about what is considered to be important in their culture. Although adults are important in supporting children and helping them to play, they are not vital in the process, as many children in different parts of the world learn how to play from other, more experienced child players. The features linked with symbolic behaviour, pretend and imagination, deepen through having opportunities for solitary play, for example, with small-world play props. In this, children can often be heard chattering away, supplying different voices for different characters.

> *Sadman found speaking English hard when he first came to St Francis School, but frequently spoke his native Bengali into the telephone. He has his diary and his pen.* (Lamb, 2002)

Another context in which we see children deep in solitary play is the way that they enjoy playing alone with constructions and how this turns into creativity and technological and engineering feats. Working out the mechanics of riding a tricycle and keeping it on the path, so that you feel in control, is the kind of exhilarating play researched by Harding (2001: 24).

Babies enjoy solitary play. The pioneering work of Goldschmied with treasure baskets full of natural objects engages sitting babies in deep play with objects.

Solitary play engages children in the deepest levels of thought and idea creation, and the most intense facing of their feelings and reflection on relationships. Knowing yourself and pushing your limits of thinking are invaluable aspects of playing alone. Personal space is a central need for young children, and perhaps for each of us in adult life too.

8 Playing together

Companionship play

This is usually referred to as parallel play, but I prefer to rename it. It means that children can, out of the corners of their eyes, see what another child or adult player is doing, and be influenced by or influence the other. Companionship play is a wonderful way of being alone in a crowd. This is comfortable play. This is why toddlers, who are just learning about symbolic play (making one thing stand for another) in the characters and stories they are beginning to create, frequently indulge in companionship play. They also get a tremendous amount of learning through heuristic play (Goldschmied and Jackson, 1994; Manning-Morton and Thorp, 2003; Forbes, forthcoming). Heuristic play is for toddlers to satisfy their urge to explore objects and find out how they behave. They need a wide variety of objects to interest them and experiment with, which are not toys.

Co-operative play

This burgeons between four and seven years of age, developing into a creative core which deepens during middle childhood. Too much adult control, domination and invasion of play, along with little time or space for it, will extinguish free-flow play. Older or more experienced players are as important as adults in developing free-flow play. A group of children involved in co-operative bike play at Greengables Nursery School, carefully adjust their movements and positioning in order to keep the play flowing. It is also important to remember that co-operative play, like solitary and companionship play, does not have to involve pretend or role play. This bike play is more scientific.

Leading and following – both matter

It is important to be aware of both children who fear loss of control and always insist on leading the play and children who are always the followers. Children need, as their co-operative play develops, to sometimes lead, sometimes follow and sometimes negotiate within the team. This helps them to become rounded people. People who can only lead are not good as team members. People who can only follow are not assertive enough, and may become passive.

9 The importance of carrying out your personal play agenda

Everyone involved in free-flow play will have their own, highly individual play agenda, which will usually be at an intuitive level. However, adults who are inclined to over-teach tend to push their agenda and see it as the most important during the play. But when each player respects and connects with the play agenda of fellow players, the free-flow play becomes rich.

Play tutoring and guided play are not free-flow play because the adult is completely dominant, excluding all the other play agendas which the children bring to the situation. These are adult-led tasks with an adult agenda. There is a place for these, but it is confusing to call them play. It is best to call them what they are: adult-led tasks.

A child might begin to play by joining the free-flow play initiated by an adult or other children. Once the process is under way, the child will introduce his or her own play agenda and develop it in co-ordination with others.

Adults can make a huge contribution to free-flow play by participating in it with the children. All an adult needs to remember if the play is to be deep and rich in quality, is that their play agenda is no more important than that of the other players. The first thing during the play is to tune into the play agendas of the children, and link theirs with them. The play will flourish. In the photograph of the sea play scenario at Prestonfield Primary School which we looked at in an earlier part of the book, the teacher participates in the play with the children, carefully tuning into their play agendas, and not 'over-teaching' (Greenman and Stonehouse, 1997: 219).

10 Being deeply involved during play

Plunging deep and wallowing in free-flow play indicates the involvement and focus children give to their play when they have time and space and helpful people to encourage it.

Concentration is a great predictor of later academic success and its beginnings. Children who concentrate though their play learn how to become engaged in their learning.

> At St Francis School, three-year-olds Connor and James are enjoying domestic play in the house corner. James is changing the doll's clothes and has the feeding bottle at the ready, and Connor prepares the meal. Both boys also frequently push their chosen dolls in the buggy and pram around the classrooms and outdoor area. Connor and James are wallowing in their free-flow play. They use the typical themes of everyday living in their play scenario.

Free-flow play makes the brain flexible and adaptable

Being able to play is a state of mind, during which the brain opens up and is at its most flexible and adaptable. Children, as they wallow in their play, become confident enough to push beyond the here-and-now and delve into the past, re-organize it and examine futures.

Playfulness

As we saw in Chapter 1, the brain, when the conditions are right, releases chemicals which open up the mind to become flexible, adaptive and imaginative. Finding out more about what helps this to happen will help children to develop the kind of play which develops into adult creativity. Garvey (1977: 12) points out that it is important to say what is and is not play. Playfulness is not play. But it does signal a move from the literal (real life) to the non-literal (play). Bateson (1955) argues that it announces the onset of play and opening up to a state of flowing thoughts that are part of playing. Playfulness is a state of mind. It opens the way for free-flow play. Free-flow play can be full of fun and laughter, but it is often very serious, dealing with grief and sadness, providing those at play are sufficiently involved and able to wallow with sufficient depth.

Opening us up to new ways of thinking

Egan (1997: 8) suggests that it is difficult for the human mind to escape from the ways of thinking that have developed in a culture. He quotes John Maynard Keynes (1936: xxiii), the economist, 'The difficulty lies, not in the new ideas, but in escaping from the old ones, which ramify, for those brought up as most of us have been, into every corner of our minds.' Undoubtedly we get into habits which hold back our thinking about developing learning through play.

Egan recognizes that there is another problem. When we escape from the conventional ideas about play, we replace the old grand narratives (as Lyotard calls them) about play with new mini-narratives for which we invent new vocabulary. Because these 'shifting stories' (Egan, 1997: 154) do not link in holistic ways with what went before, they often go off on completely different and much narrower paths of exploration. The word playfulness is one of these narrow paths. It has become widely used because of the postmodern influences in early childhood education. Egan (1997: 154) says: 'Pointless, purposeless activity is, after all, how play used to be defined until its fundamental psychological and social importance became clear, and postmodernists happily adopt this sense of playfulness.'

Being more than playful

To imply that the only point of play is that it lacks purpose is too narrow because this focuses on one aspect of play in isolation from other equally important features. Playfulness, as we have seen, is a signal that play is about to flow. It alerts others that there is to be a shift from the state of real life to the state of free-flow play and all that is involved. Children often make an announcement, such as 'Let's play monsters!', as they move into an imaginative play scenario. Rough and tumble play often signals this too. Adults move into playfulness when they initiate play with a baby, with exaggerated gestures, facial expressions and movements, as if to say, let's move from ordinary living into free-flow play.

The central issue is that play brings the open-mindedness, flexibility and agility of mind which is fundamental to creativity, and the possibility for this developing is seen in the way the different features of play co-ordinate with each other. This is different from those isolated postmodern 'shifting stories' that fleetingly describe the latest fashions about play until a new story ousts them. Meade (2002) asks of her colleagues in New Zealand whether early childhood practitioners are ready for the 'shifting stories' and vocabularies of postmodernism.

Fortunately, it does not have to be a case of postmodernism compared with the Enlightenment. Postmodernists dismiss what they see as the Enlightenment notion that there can be any universal ways of exploring concepts such as play. Whilst rejecting the Enlightenment view that there are universals in relation to the concept of play, Egan (1997: 154) suggests that there are, nevertheless, areas of solidarity between those holding different perspectives on the concept of play. The notion of areas of solidarity is similar to the scientific view that different evidence from diverse research and data often results in converging evidence, which leads to convincing evidence about the importance of play in childhood.

11 Demonstrating recent learning, skills and competencies

Play is not so much about new learning as using what you have learned. It is about the application of knowledge and ideas, and what has been understood about feelings, relationships and how to use body movement with skill. Children who know something well will begin to play using humour.
(Athey, 1990)

Consolidating learning

Free-flow play allows children to consolidate their learning so that it becomes embedded. This is very different from the kind of dreary repetitive exercises found on worksheets or lists of endlessly similar sums to be practised. Play allows children to repeat things, but in a constantly flowing context. Hebb (1961) described this as the 'difference in the sameness'. This keeps the interest and motivation high. Playing house with one group of children on one day will be entirely different from playing with different children another day. This demands flexibility so that nothing is an exact repeat, even if play scenarios have the same theme. Playing with jumping is entirely different on grass, a bouncy castle or tarmac.

Demonstrating competencies

Children demonstrate technical prowess, riding a two-wheel bicycle, writing a shopping list when playing shops, being different characters. An older child might skilfully help younger children to join in the play without disrupting it, yet keeping the play theme going with all the players participating with a depth of satisfaction.

The children of Charles and Emma Darwin were very well educated, because they were encouraged to learn through play, and to reason and understand their learning, which took place indoors and outdoors, rather than in a schoolroom learning grammar exercises by rote, and copywriting. The Darwins were influenced by the principles of the educational pioneer, Johan Pestalozzi (1746–1827). Both the governess, Miss Thorley, and Emma Darwin (mother) would join the children in their play sometimes. A favourite piece of play was on a slide. A friend wrote:

> *This toy, to use an unworthy and inadequate name, has a place in every Darwin household, but I have never seen one anywhere else. It consists simply in a long strip of polished wood with protecting edges and a small flange at one end by which it can be hooked on to any step of the staircase that the slider, in his timidity or bravery, desires. It is possible to invent various feats of fancy sliding – sitting, standing, or head-first, but the ultimate test of skill and courage was always 'eight steps standing'.* (Keynes, 2002: 105)

Applying learning

Darwin's children provide many examples of technical prowess in the application of their knowledge and understanding. Annie, his eldest daughter, used to play at making collections, having observed her father at work in his study.

> *Annie liked to name the precise colours of things she found and often imitated her father by matching objects with the colour samples in a small book he had used for describing specimens during his travels on HMS Beagle. Werner's Nomenclature of Colours edited by Patrick Syme, a flower painter in Edinburgh, gave a set of colour samples with names, and for each, offered a list of examples in different parts of the natural world, animal, vegetable and mineral. Charles would have been able to show Annie the minerals from his collection of specimens. Many of the other things she knew in the garden and countryside around the house.* (Keynes, 2002: 103)

The important thing here is that children observe their parents and family and adults at work, in shops, with hobbies and in recreational activities. They incorporate what they learn into their play and apply their learning as they do so. Annie's play showed how deeply she understood what her father had taught her about nature study.

Brandon watching TV

12 Play as an integrating mechanism

Play helps children to become whole people and it helps children to be balanced, having a sense of well-being. Play is also an organizing principle which co-ordinates and orchestrates what has been learnt, so that learning has meaning and can be effectively used in different situations with different people.

Play, according to Stuart Brown, who as a clinician in a hospital has undertaken years of painstaking data-gathering from more than 8,000 subjects, including children with rubella, male murderers, male serial drunken drivers and gifted men, found that: 'normal play behaviour was virtually absent throughout the lives of highly violent, antisocial men regardless of demography. Although physical abuse and social (largely paternal) deprivations were significant in predicting chronic risks for violence in the homicide studies, in both the drunken antisocial drivers and the murderers absent or clearly abnormal play was in league with later social and personal tragedy.'

Play is a strong determining factor in preventing children from later 'social and personal tragedy' (Bekoff and Byers, 1998: 249). It is good for individuals to experience play as children, but it is also good for society because it means that children do not become violent, antisocial adults. Play helps people's minds to be organized, so that they can become good thinkers, and it also leads to a sense of well-being and good relationships with others.

Getting to the essentials of play

Free-flow play deeply involves children so that they wallow and reach their greatest levels of concentration. This involves their ideas, thoughts, feelings, relationships and physical movements. Free-flow play enables children to apply what they know, reflect on it, use it in different ways, experiment and explore with what they know and have learnt of relationships, feelings, ideas, thought and the movement of their bodies.

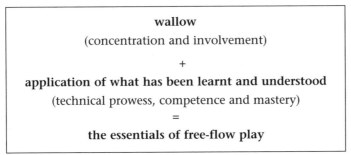

wallow
(concentration and involvement)

+

application of what has been learnt and understood
(technical prowess, competence and mastery)

=

the essentials of free-flow play

The ability to wallow, be involved in play, focus and concentrate deeply, together with competent, skilled and masterly application of knowledge and understanding is at the heart of play, but surrounding its heart are the other features which identify it as play rather than anything else. All of the 12 features make up the whole, and these ideas are continually evolving into new understandings about play. Play is not a static concept. Just as the children's play flows and changes, so the theory is in a state of flow, continuing into adulthood. Play is a birth to death concept.

In practice

- Do you find that children need your help getting into a state of free-flow play?
- If a child is in a group, and another announces 'We're playing shops', and the child stands, not knowing what to do, do you point out that Sharon has picked up a shopping bag, and Jo likes the cash register, and Jess is making money out of beads and putting them in her purse. This gives the child some ideas without imposing one on them.
- Do you observe play?
- How do you evaluate what you offer to support and extend play?
- How do you assess the play of individual children? If seven or more of the 12 features of free-flow play are present, the learning through play is probably developing well.
- Do you know much about the play of the children you work with? If play really is the highest form of a child's learning, it is important to know that all the children you work with are developing their play. This is important for principles of inclusion and the equalities. Inclusion means that every child feels they matter, and that they belong to the group. This does not mean that everyone has to be the same, or to be treated in the same way. One size does not fit all. This applies to issues of gender, ethnicity, creed, disability, special educational needs, English as an additional language, age (such as being one of the youngest children in a group) physical size, economic background, geographic area, health. Every child is an individual, with individual needs, as well as being a member of the human race, and part of their family, group or communities. Is the child's development in play a valued part of your record-keeping?

Further reading

Bruce, T. (1997) *Early Childhood Education*, 2nd edn. London: Hodder and Stoughton.

Bruce, T. (1996) *Helping Young Children to Play*. London: Hodder and Stoughton.

Bruce, T. (2001a) *Learning Through Play: Babies, Toddlers and the Foundation Years*. London: Hodder and Stoughton.

Gura, P., ed. (1992) *Exploring Learning: Young Children and Blockplay*. London: Paul Chapman Publishing.

Jenkinson, S. (2002) *The Genius of Play: Celebrating the Spirit of Childhood*. Hawthorn Press.

Kalliala, M. (In press) *Children's Play Culture in a Changing World*. Maidenhead: Open University Press.

Long, A. (2001) 'Forget about the "music" – Concentrate on the Children', *Early Childhood Practice: The Journal for Multi-Professional Partnerships* 3(1): 71–6.

10

Using symbols

Key themes

Symbols stand for things. People become able to think more deeply, flexibly and in the abstract as they begin to develop their understanding of symbols. From the time they are toddlers, they begin to tease out how to make different kinds of symbols, and how other people make and use them.

In this way, they begin to understand that they can be creative, and find and make their own personal symbols. Alongside this, they begin to explore, decode and make use of the symbols central to the culture in which they grow up.

Becoming a symbol user means that a young child develops symbolic layerings, which deepen the ability to think about the past, present and future. In doing so, children develop their ideas, thoughts and maturity of emotions (sometimes called emotional intelligence), and their relationships with others benefit.

It is important to note that symbol use also involves the physical development and learning of a child. Using a paintbrush, dancing, singing and using musical instruments, mark-making and model-making, constructing with wooden blocks all involve physical co-ordination.

Children take great joy in becoming symbol users, providing their personal symbols are valued, and provided they are not forced into early and inappropriate adult-led tasks so that conventional symbols squeeze out their own. When this happens, meaning is lost, and the tasks are arid and wearisome for young children. We must not be destructive of the child's biological propensity for becoming a symbol user. Instead, we need to cultivate the disposition to make and use symbols.

A teddy bear is often a very precious thing to a young child. The head teacher at Cameron House showed her teddy to the children. She wanted to give them a sense of time passing and introduce them to history. She had loved this teddy when she was a little girl, and had kept it across the years. Here the teddy is a symbol that is easy to understand for young children in order to grasp the passing of time.

A home-made book

Several children were very interested to discuss this. Ellis told his mother about the conversation, and his mother made him a book at home about his teddy. The title was 'My Teddy'.

On the inside cover:
His mother has made a letter E out of buttons, and there are photographs of him playing with the teddy on a see-saw in the park.

The second page says:
Teddies must be safe on our journeys, all strapped in. I'm looking after them. There is a photograph of two of his teddies strapped into a car seat with the safety strap.

The third page says:
At home with our favourite teddy.
Two photographs are framed with wooden lollypop sticks, showing him with the teddy.

The fourth page says:
Time to tuck teddy in bed as I read my favourite book.
There is a photograph framed with coloured plastic strips.

The fifth page says:
Showing Baby Blue (the name of the teddy) all the fantastic pictures.
There is a photograph of him in bed looking at a picture book.

The sixth page says:
We are all tired. Time to say 'Night-night'.
The photograph is of him asleep in bed with his teddy, framed with plastic strips.

The last page says:
Sleeping like a diamond in the sky. Sweet dreams.
The picture is framed with plastic diamonds, circles, triangles and semi-circles.
There is an arrow to one of the diamond shapes.

Powerful emotional messages

This book was made with loving care. Perhaps it brought back memories of mother's teddy which she had had as a child. Teddies often carry feelings of comfort, safeness, and the times when we feel very loved. Symbols are imbued with meaning and the books we give children about them, and make with them, have emotional as well as intellectual meaning, which is why they are so powerful; they reactivate episodic memories.

Children beginning to be symbol users
Non-verbal forms of symbol use

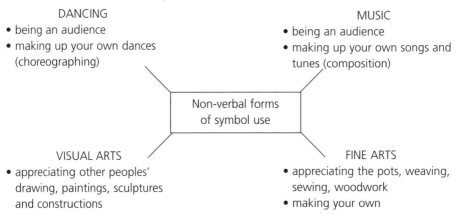

DANCING
- being an audience
- making up your own dances (choreographing)

MUSIC
- being an audience
- making up your own songs and tunes (composition)

Non-verbal forms of symbol use

VISUAL ARTS
- appreciating other peoples' drawing, paintings, sculptures and constructions
- creating your own

FINE ARTS
- appreciating the pots, weaving, sewing, woodwork
- making your own

Throughout the book, we see children participating in their culture, and engaged in emergent forms of non-verbal symbol use.

Given opportunities and encouragement, even very young children begin to explore and find out ways of keeping hold of experiences. It is easier to keep a pot, or woodwork construction than it is to keep a dance or tune to share and use on another day. Simple forms of dance and music notation are possible. A row of dots might be early efforts to write a musical rhythm. Children also experiment with writing numbers and letters.

Children both problem-solve and problem-generate in relation to their earlier use of symbols of all kinds.

If children are given the opportunities, they begin to find out ways of keeping hold of experiences (representing them) through:

- Dance notation: finding ways of writing down the dances you make so that you can share them and dance them again on another day.
- Mathematical: other people's written symbol conventions for numbers, geometry and algebra; problem-solving and problem-generating, writing down mathematical problems and solutions in a spirit of adventure.

Symbols using written words

1. Literature: being read to, and beginning to get to know about people's stories, rhymes and poems, and accessing information.
2. Literacy: beginning to write for yourself – information, stories, rhymes and poems.
3. Musical literacy notation: learning about how people write down songs or music so as to keep it, remember it and perform it again.
4. Musical notation: writing down songs and musical compositions that you want to write for yourself.

Personal and conventional symbols

Every child is part of the culture in which he or she grows up. However, as we have seen, children need to have the opportunity to experiment with the symbols they find other people using as part of the process of beginning to understand and use them in their dances, music-making, drawings, paintings, models, mathematical experiments, literary and literacy adventures. As children participate in their culture, they find themselves, and hopefully experiment with and develop their own personal style of writing, taste in reading and artistic self.

People who can only be the audience of other people's stories, mathematical problems, visual experiments, dances and music are unlikely to be creative, imaginative, or have fulfilling expressive and intellectual lives. Children deserve better than to copy what others do for the whole of their lives. A. Maslow, a psychologist, wrote: 'If you deliberately plan to be less than you are capable of being, then I warn you that you will be deeply unhappy for the rest of your life. You will be evading your possibilities.' (Maslow, 1987: 40)

Because human beings are capable of being symbol users in ways which no animals achieve, it is important that we encourage our children in this respect.

It is important not to insist on children only using the conventional symbols, and encourage them to use their own personal symbols so as to gain control over the way they develop their understanding and use of conventional ones. If children lose their ability to make personal symbols, as well as to develop the use of conventional ones they lose the possibility of becoming creative, imaginative symbol users.

The staff at the Craigmillar Children's Centre are working to take the children's interests as the starting-point, and are helping children to make con-

nections with diverse areas of learning, rather than using the children's interests only as a way of making them fit the adults' agenda.

The following extract from the staff's notes shows how this is progressing.

When Eddie got stuck in the traffic

*Many of the children in the playroom for the three to five year olds expressed
an interest in adult roles and 'work'. They were particularly keen to find out
what the different people who work within the Children's Centre do. Eddie, the
unit's bus driver/handy person, is a very popular figure and the children often
enquire about his role.*

*One of the members of staff invented a song which is sung to the tune of
'When Santa got stuck up the chimney'. This song proved very popular with
the children and is often a first choice at singing time. Children from other
rooms also sing the song.*

*It was decided by staff that owing to the children's great interest, the song
should be developed into a book.*

*Eddie kindly agreed to become involved and work began on the book. The
children helped to choose the pictures which were to accompany each line of
the song and the pictures which were to accompany the format of the book,
which was made in the shape of a bus, with large print.*

*We have been singing the song with the children so that we can develop our
own 'When Eddie got stuck in the traffic' song tape.*

The staff at Craigmillar Children's Centre say: 'Our project is still very much a
work in progress. We intend to continue to develop our ideas with the children.
We have recently purchased a children's camera and intend to assist the children in taking their own photographs and making their own books, special to
them.'

The challenge for the staff is to resist the temptation to design books which
are about the adults' agenda of what should be in them. However, the staff
began with a very adult-led approach to the books.

*Our project was developed from an interest in the use of photographic images
as a means of enhancing learning opportunities. We designed a variety of
books and activities using photographs and pictorial images.*

Staff are finding the value of moving away from inappropriate adult-led
tasks. Instead, they are letting children take photographs and begin to initiate their own conversations about their snapshots, which often lead to fascinating discussions of exactly those things.

Staff are also moving away from using books as an opportunity to give children exercises in matching words, and instead are helping children to take photographs of new children settling into the nursery, and to see the staff working in the nursery. This leads to conversations which link with all areas of learning in the curriculum.

Whitehead (2002) writes about the importance of having what she calls 'community narratives' like these. No one outside this community would know about the important part that Eddie is playing in the lives of children and families attending the Craigmillar Children's Centre. Not all of these community narratives are written down, but whether they are sung together or written down in shared books, they play an important role in developing a sense of belonging. Children love to look at photograph books with simple text that encourages them to feel they belong.

Encouraging parents to enjoy helping their children become symbol users

At Greendykes Children's Centre staff have been involved in two projects, 'All about me' and 'Fred the Ted'. Here we see the way in which parents are encouraged to use the much loved toys of their children, such as teddies, to begin to develop symbol use in deeper and deeper layers with their children. '"Fred the Ted" was introduced to develop links between home and Greendykes Children's Centre, to share experiences and feelings, to encourage language and literacy and to develop self esteem and confidence.' (Staff comment, Greendykes Children's Centre, 2002).

The children take it in turns to take Fred the Ted home with them for the weekend. The family record what adventures Fred has with the family, and this is shared at group time with the other children.

Here are some examples of Fred's adventures. He is not always mentioned, but he is there for the whole weekend with Gemma.

Hello everyone. This is Gemma's story.
Friday 16th February
I brought Fred home today and I gave him a big cuddle. Auntie Carol came to my house. Her pet name for me is Daisy Bell. She loves me very much.

Saturday 17th February
My Nana came along to take me to her house. She reads lots of stories our of my books. Nan has a cat called Balgheera but I cant say that so I

call him Baga. He is a lovely cat.

Sunday 18th February
I am at my Nana's today. Again she took pictures of me in her bed. I
was playing with the mouth organ and Nana was dancing to the music.
I will finish my story now.
Love Gemma

Here we see Gemma's family entering into the spirit of telling Fred's story,
and using some of the conventions of writing. The diary is written in the first
person ('I am at my Nana's today') and it has a clear beginning and ending
('This is Gemma's story', and 'Love Gemma'). All of this introduces Gemma
to book language, which she will need as a reader and writer. It does so, as
the book 'My Teddy' did, in a way which links with Gemma's own experiences. It is a powerful literary experience because of that.

   In the next outing that Fred makes, to Conor's home, we see how Fred
really becomes part of the story and a character. These two elements, the
story-line and the characters, are of fundamental importance in creative
writing. If children have 'lived' these kinds of play scenario they know about
the mechanics of story-making.

Friday, 17th August
Fred is welcomed into Conor's household for the weekend. Fred is
introduced to Conor's big sister, Emma, little sister Dayna and Mum.
Mum takes all of us to visit Nana and Gramps in Danderhall. Fred sits on
my knee with the seatbelt around him, so I know he is safe. We arrive
at Nan and Gramps and Nana hugs and kisses Fred. We then go to the
swing park where we have lots of fun. Nana gets over excited with the
camera and takes lots of pictures of us with Fred. After the swing park
we go shopping for the tea then home. Fred shares Conor's dinner, then
Conor washes his face. Conor puts Fred in the ironing basket to sleep as
it is soft on top of the clothes.

Saturday 18th August
Fred and Conor gets up long before Mummy opens her eyes. We all
have breakfast. Fred really enjoyed his cornflakes. He then sits on the
potty and gets washed. Mummy takes us out.

The nursery and primary schools in this book met with the local secondary schools, and revised and agreed ways forward in cultivating literacy so that children are encouraged develop and experiment with personal symbols alongside experimenting with and beginning to develop understanding of the conventional writing symbols and signs.

They emphasized the importance of ensuring that all children have the best possible opportunities to achieve their linguistic possibilities, and are not pushed early or rigidly into the conventions of writing and reading.

The Castlebrae Cluster's key principles for literacy

- To foster a positive, stimulating environment which nurtures confidence, self-esteem and motivation throughout the community
- To encourage, value and support parental involvement and partnership strategies within the community
- To promote literacy as pleasurable, relevant, worthwhile and of lifelong importance
- To accord literacy high status within each setting and throughout school
- To provide through a variety of approaches, strategies and resources differentiated language experiences which meet individual needs
- To have high expectations which value and extend previous experiences
- To ensure a strong literacy focus in the early years which takes account of linguistic and cognitive development
- To maintain and extend a continuing programme of high-quality staff development
- To promote the right of every child to access early education delivered by appropriately trained staff
- To prioritize the resourcing of literacy development in terms of personnel and materials

---

Early reading

The first words children read

The first words children learn to read are words that have emotional and intellectual meaning for them. Their name, the name of other people, pets, objects they love or are interested in, are often the first words they try to write and read. One of the greatest factors in lifting children to be good readers and writers is the extent to which parents are interested and involved in this with their children (Athey, 1990; Whalley, 2001; Siraj-Blatchford, 2002).

Research suggests that the book the mother made about the teddy will have far more impact on the child's pleasure in books and desire to read them than formal instruction in phonics. Whitehead (1999: 55) notes that during group instruction in phonics a few children at the front: 'enjoy the teacher's performance and manage a little interaction, but many who are further away drift off into contemplation of a spider under the window sill, or the writing on the T-shirt of the child next to them, or go in for more disruptive activities. This comes as no surprise to students of child development.'

Building on what is known of the way the children develop, Whitehead believes that the most effective way to share reading and writing with children, so that they engage in these symbolic activities by themselves gradually, is to focus on:

- making of meanings;
- the narrative (story) and how to make stories together, like the 'My Teddy' book;
- how the layers of print, pictures and lay-out of both work together to help the reader;
- how real experiences (with teddies) link with literary experiences (such as the story of 'Dogger' by Shirley Hughes);
- writing to turn children's ideas, feelings and experiences into the written word;
- showing children the conventions of print symbols, such as letters, words, sentences, question marks, full stops;
- helping children, with adult support, to behave like writers, and make decisions and choose what they want to say, and to have a go without fear of getting it wrong.

What is involved in reading

Semantics

Children need to make sense of what they read and write.

Syntax

Unless children can speak the language of the text with enough experience and proficiency, they will not be able to make sense of what they read, or write with any success. Spoken language comes before writing and reading.

Grapho-phonics

The look of the letters, words and sentences and the relationships of letters to the sounds they make are a crucial part of learning to read. Children cannot make use of the relationship between sounds and the look of letters if these are taught in isolation from a meaningful context. Music, rhymes and poetry facilitate phonological awareness (or the organization of sound).

Vocabulary (lexicon)

Children who are confident communicators, with plenty to say and the words they need to express their ideas, feelings and relationships, enjoy books and read and write more easily. Spoken language makes a huge contribution to how a child makes a start on writing and reading.

Becoming a reader

Children develop layers of symbolic behaviours as they become readers. Gardner (1993) calls these layers different 'waves' of symbolic behaviour. With each layer or wave of symbolic behaviour, the child is able to deepen the use of symbols at increasingly complex levels.

We saw in Chapter 1 how even babies love books. The Craigmillar Books for Babies Project makes an important contribution to the earliest symbolic layerings, using picture books. Babies appreciate picture images, and as we have seen, these continue to be important until children are well established, usually in the later part of the primary school, in their reading and writing fluency.

Indeed, adults also appreciate pictures to support many of the texts they read. Being read to is crucial in enjoying books. Reading alone develops only as children become very fluent readers, and children who continue to be read to until the end of the junior school tackle more difficult texts because of this. This takes us to Vygotsky's (1978) theory of potential development, which shows that what we can do with help today, we shall be able to do alone and independently tomorrow.

The first layer of symbolic behaviour – beginning to read and write

Children work out what text is, and how it works. They sort out where the story begins, and where it ends, and how to deal with the bits in the middle.

Ellis, who made the book about the teddy with his mother, loves to keep returning to it, but he needs his mother to read it for him. He is fascinated that the things they have talked about together can be represented in a book, with words written down in print.

He will often go and find this book, and 'read' it with reading-like behaviour again and again and again. He almost knows the book by heart as he has memorized what the words say, and he uses the pictures as important cues.

It is very helpful to him that the text is so easy for him to relate to his own experiences. This is the value of having a book that has been made specially for him. Books need to allow children to bring their own experiences to the text, and they need to be encouraged to talk with adults or other children about this.

The second layer of symbolic behaviour – becoming an emergent reader

Being able to predict what the writing says

Children, as they hear stories again and again, and find favourites in the book corner, begin to realize that a text, either fictional, about a story, poem or rhyme, or non-fictional, giving information, is consistent and does not alter. The pictures help the emergent reader to understand the text, and to talk around it, but the words do not change. 'We are all tired. Time to say Night-night.' Familiar, favourite books help children as they begin to self-correct as they read. Such books have short, manageable sentences.

Encouraging sound and letter combinations

This means that children need help to learn that the name for a letter is different from how it will sound in different words. This develops best when situations crop up spontaneously, rather than through herding children into adult-set tasks, which often de-motivate young children quite quickly.

Phonological awareness

It is very helpful for children if they are offered rhymes, poems and songs (Goswami and Bryant, 1990). Whitehead (2002: 39) says, 'Regular patterns can be heard in the beginning of words and when these are the same we call them alliteration. Repeated and similar-sounding endings are called rhyme.' 'Ted' and 'bed' rhyme. The adult might make up a rhyming song along the lines of:

Come on Ted,
It's time for bed.

Or on another occasion the adult might use alliteration:

A toothbrush for Ted
Ttttttttttttttttttttttttttttttttttt
Yes
Here it is
A toothbrush for Ted!

Children delight in making up simple songs and rhymes with adults. They are of central importance because, as Whitehead (2002: 39) warns, 'Many poor readers in primary schools are remarkably insensitive to rhymes and to the beginning sounds of words.'

It is important to bear in mind that children become avid emergent readers only if the beginnings of reading have gone well for them. The adult-led task orientation of early formal teaching of reading and writing has a tendency to leave out the beginning reading part of the process, and this often results in children becoming dutiful emergent readers rather than avid emergent readers. When this happens children are well on the way to 'barking' at print and only reading when duty requires. The sensitive help that a child receives is more likely to turn him or her into a bookworm in the later part of primary school, and hopefully for the rest of his or her life.

The children at Greengables are supported as beginning and emergent readers in ways which help them to develop the strategies they will need in becoming confident, fluent readers and writers beyond the call of duty, and because they need and want to read and write for themselves as well as for others.

The children are offered rich experiences with books, both fiction and non-fiction. They have begun to gain a good idea of what book language sounds like, because it is quite different from spoken language.

Encouraging children to use a wide range of symbols

Children at Greengables have plenty of opportunities for mark-making. This gives sound beginnings for later writing as well as for two-dimensional art (drawing and painting).

Mark making at Greengables

In the photographs you can see children making marks which are letter-like as well as representing people and other things. The outdoor learning environment encourages this as much as the indoor provision.

A group of children at Greengables were taken to visit the office where Lee's mother worked. She showed them round, and explained some of the work they did, using the computer, internet and printer. Lee sat on his mum's swivel chair in front of her computer. The children were struck by the size of the building, which even had shops in it, and the fact that they could ride on an escalator to get round inside the building more quickly. They loved stopping on their tour of the building to have juice and biscuits in the cafeteria. The group of four children also visited the Craigmillar Festival Society office.

On return to Greengables, the children visited the office of the secretary, Rosemary. They used the photocopier, fax machine and computer.

By now they had experienced three different offices. Then the children, helped by the adults, made their own office. After the summer holidays, the interest did not fade. The children who had been on the original visit were now the older children in their second year of the nursery school. They brought their experiences of the summer into the nursery. Some of the boys and girls had gone away in the summer holidays. Somebody had been to Florida. Someone else had been to Gran Canaria.

The interest in offices remained at Greengables after the summer holidays, and the children turned the office into a travel agent's, with help from the staff. It is important to stress that this would not have been possible if staff had not been committed to observing and responding to children's interests.

The best teaching is informed by observation of children's interests, which is acted on and supported and extended by the adults working with the children (DFES, 2000). The real experience of visiting offices led to the representation of office experiences afterwards. Helping children to create such play scenarios develops rich symbol use by the children, broad and rich in its variety.

Here are some of the activities the children took part in.

- Role play: the office play scenario
- Transforming the graphics area into an office
- Small world play: the train set
- Relevant commercial books
- Making their own books and play props
- Having a go at writing and reading
- Really cooking pizza
- Pretend imaginative cooking of pizza and pasta with play dough
- Making passports for the play scenario
- Construction with large hollow blocks: a car

Not only did the staff help the children transform the office into a travel agency, but a group of children also went to Waverley Station in Edinburgh by train. After the visit, some of the children enjoyed playing with the small world train tracks. Here is another kind of symbolic layer. We have reading, writing, small-world play and larger role play in the office.

Importance of adults

All the differing symbolic layerings here help each other along. The narratives (stories) which develop through these play scenarios form the basis of later creative writing. Because adults make displays and books with the children about the visits, the stories do not escape, but are turned into fiction and non-fiction books. This is a print-rich environment. It is more than that though. It is also a symbol-rich environment. Given that it is the symbolic life of a culture which makes humans what they are, this is an important part of the way we live with and work with young children.

The important thing to remember is that children are biologically and socially inclined to want to understand symbols and also to use them for themselves. If we as adults force the deepest layers of symbolic behaviour on them, through the transmission-style teaching of early reading and writing, before they have firmly grasped and begun to use previous symbolic layerings, we actually make it more difficult for them rather than easier.

Many children are easily put off. They then become at worst refusers, or reluctant, dutiful symbol users (especially in reading and writing) rather than the confident, enthusiastic and increasingly skilled symbol users that children are capable of becoming.

Using symbols in role play scenarios

As the interest in the travel agent's developed, the staff encouraged the children by making an attractive area for them to develop their ideas. The travel agent's was often very busy.

Michael decided to book a holiday to Italy at the Greengables Travel Agent, so he looked it up on the internet. Some of the children made pizza, a favourite Italian meal. Connor was a new boy, attending full-time in the nursery. Being busy in the travel agent's and cooking pizza helped him to settle in. Michael's mum came in to help with snacks on the day pizza was made at Greengables.

Michael invited Mrs. M into the home corner where he was making some food. He said, 'Do you want to go to Italy?' He then handed Mrs M a passport and said, 'You'll need that for Italy.' He asked what food they ate in Italy and Mrs. M said that they ate lots of pasta. M. then made plates of pasta (from play dough) and enjoyed learning some Italian words. The pasta was, 'bell', bella'. He was very amused by all this. (Staff observation, Greengables 2002)

The children's end-of-term outing was to Purves Puppets. The children were booking themselves in using the travel agent's to do so. Michael used the phone, and Connor sold tickets. He told people: 'The show starts at five'.

Michael, Connor and Taylor all used the office, with lots of interest in the phones, hole punch and other office equipment.

Taylor and Michael, using the phone between each other:
Taylor – I'm in my office.
Michael – Are you coming to mine?
Taylor orders her lunch over the phone, taking notes on the paper.
Michael uses small pieces of paper to swipe through the paper rack.
Connor mounts card on to paper to post to 'Derek the fireman'. (Staff observation, Greengables, 2002)

The office-like behaviours, based on real experience of offices, is helping the children to develop deeper layerings of symbolic behaviour. It helps them to make stories, read and write, and use technology.

The next observations shows us further developments.

The keyboard had been moved into the office. Taylor and Kelsey moved their chairs from the desk to the keyboard when they needed to type. Taylor showed Mrs. M. a piece of paper with 'writing on' which had, 'come out of my machine'. (Sticky tape is being used at the moment to stick the phone and hole punch.) Kelsey put some paper into the slot in the keyboard so that it stood up. Michael asked what the sharpener was for and how to use it.
Dillan used the phone dictionary, 'To look up numbers'.
Dionne used the hard-backed book to write pages of letters. Taylor wrote a notelet and used a magnet to stick it to the radiator, as did Kimberley. (Staff observation, Greengables, 2002)

Staff suspect that it may have been the activity at the travel agent's that made the children want to read and write more. But not only were the children enthused. Mrs Brock decided that she might go away on holiday next year and she would need a passport. Mrs Brock showed Michael how to fill in a

Suddenly Michael wants to write numbers!

passport application form. They went to the photo booth so that she could get a passport photo taken. Some of the other children wanted their own passports, so the staff helped them. They also had photos. This was a very popular activity.

Steven and Michael went to the local post office to get a stamp, so that Mrs Brock's application for a passport could be sent.

Michael

It is particularly interesting to follow Michael in detail. His symbolic behaviour has a huge influence on his learning in every area. In this staff observation, we see him involved in imaginative play, role play and pretend elements. This is because he rehearses adult roles, but he also pretends the blocks are different parts of the car. He consistently uses what he knows of reading and writing in his play.

Outside … Michael again engaging in imaginative play which has carried on from Friday, – driving his bus to Italy. He is sitting on the large mat surrounded by some of the large plastic blocks. He is using the old steering wheel, making appropriate noises and inviting other children and staff on to the bus. As Connor passes by in the small car (and other children on bikes) he tells me that they are other buses. He says 'Hi mate' and puts up his thumb. He also winks ('That's what drivers do!').

He uses a yellow cube with a cylinder coming out of it as his hand-brake. He then places three cubes in front of his feet, 'One's for going faster and one's for slowing down.' He is told the correct name for the pedals. Later, he says: 'I don't use the horn if someone's in the way. I just use the brake to slow down.'

Michael's imaginative play had previously been extended in the play room. We had had Italian food for snack (he had made a pizza). We had looked at the globe to see where Italy was. We had discussed how he would cross the sea. We had looked in brochures to see where we would all like to go.

When I asked Michael the next day what pedal he would press to make the bus go faster, he said, 'The accelerator'. (Staff observation, Greengables, 2002)

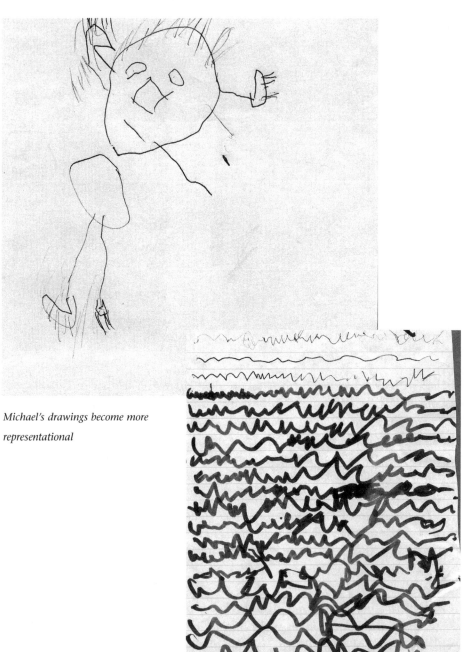

Michael's drawings become more
representational

Michael's writing about holidays

Staff at Greengables also note that 'We are beginning to see that a child steeped in symbolism, at home and in the nursery setting (well supported by experienced and appropriately trained staff) is likely to want to write down his own experiences.' They are thinking in particular of Michael here.

Creating an environment which encourages children to become symbol users

Some environments are more conducive than others to the development of symbolic behaviour, in which children are actively encouraged to develop their learning of musical and dance notation, drawings, paintings, writing, reading (literacy) and mathematical symbols, including numbers.

A book corner

This needs to be situated so that it is warm, light and cosy. Books should include poetry, fictional stories, song books with musical notation, non-fictional reference books, home-made books and staff-made books, all in clearly signalled and labelled sections. There should be a comfortable feeling, with cushions to loll on, easy chairs and an adult-sized sofa for small groups to gather and share a book together. A low table and chair is also helpful for some children. The flooring should be a rug which is comfortable to sit on.

The walls

These should not be so crowded that they are just a mass of confusion. Everything should be there for a good reason. The key message is that less is more. This means that print should be at child height and meaningful for the children. A label such as 'door' on the door is not nearly so helpful as a photograph of a child putting on a coat, which has a speech bubble saying something like, 'Is it cold outside? Do you need a coat?' If words are in context, but given meaning in this way, children begin to try to read the notices, which should contain genuine questions and information.

A few notices might be at adult height and addressed to adults. This might be the long-term plan for parents, reminders about a parents' evening or messages, such as a request for cardboard boxes for use in the workshop area. These are best kept to a clearly defined notice board.

Labels on the equipment

These help children to become familiar with important words for reading and writing. When these are with a picture, this is even more helpful. Children quickly learn to look at them when finding what they need, or when tidying things away into drawers, shelves or cupboards.

Honest labels on displays

These will be more likely to encourage children to be confident symbol users across a variety of media. If children have simply followed an adult task, and coloured in an adult's outline with paint, it is not true to say, 'We made a painting of the fire-engine'. 'We' did not; the adult did, using the children as assistants.

The labels on the display of the office project at Greengables, or the hospital project at Children's House, or the 'Long, Long Ago' project at Cameron House were designed so that the learning of the children is recorded to share with the parents and community. They also act as a reminder to individual children of their own learning.

When adults turn the children's symbolic representations (drawings and paintings, for example) into their own montage, cutting up the children's work and making it into their own collage, they are stopping children thinking for themselves and developing their ideas, thoughts, feelings and relationships with themselves, others or their universe, as they develop into confident symbol users. Imagine how Van Gogh would have felt if he found someone had cut out his picture of a chair, and mounted it in a picture labelled, 'This is the chair Goldilocks sat on in the story of the three bears'.

Long, long ago – developing an understanding of historic time using dressing up clothes as symbols of the past

At Cameron House Nursery School, Ellis started the interest the children took up in what happened long ago. He asked questions of the adults, such as 'A very long time ago, who looked after the first people on earth?'

Time is a very difficult concept to understand. The staff realized that they would need to take a very practical approach to helping Ellis and other children who were fascinated with these kinds of question. The headteacher took the teddy bear she had as a child, and showed it to the children, and this led to further discussion of the past. We saw above that Ellis brought his teddy bear to nursery school, and at home his mother made a book about it called 'My Teddy'.

Parents and staff brought in the teddies they had had as children, 'long, long ago'. They took in photographs of themselves as children, sometimes with their teddies. 'We looked at old photos and wondered about them. The children prepared afternoon tea for an elderly neighbour who visited to share with us her own photos of long ago.' (Note from a display)

Studying the past

This led staff to show the children the stained-glass windows which are part of the school building. 'Our nursery features stained glass windows by William Wilson, which tell the story of a day in the life of children at play.' (Note from a display)

Staff began to realize that this was an opportunity both to follow children's interests in 'long, long ago', and to introduce children to Scottish culture in the curriculum. The Scottish symbols help children to participate in their culture in practical ways and so develop symbolic behaviour relating to the past as well as the present. Learning about the past, using symbols of clothing and other artefacts, helps children of any culture to become symbol users. Symbols help us to understand the past, present and future. This example is of Scottish heritage, but the principle of listing historic places and re-enacting events of daily living can be applied to any culture, as Trevarthen notes in the introduction to the book.

The display boards, with photographs and notes, shared and reflected the culture with parents as well as the children, so that the whole community could learn together:

- Scottish songs are fun to sing and often tell us stories of Scottish life
- Having fun with Scottish stories – traditional and modern
- Enjoying traditional Scottish poetry ... creating some of our own!
- Creating our own songs and poetry
- Dancing to the skirl o' the pipes!

Learning about history and heritage

A piper visited, wearing traditional costume, joined by parents and children doing the same. The dressing-up took off, and so staff expanded the dressing-up clothes to encourage children to create play scenarios of 'long, long ago'. They organized a visit to Gladlands House, the home of a seventeenth-century merchant in Edinburgh. Children wore historic costume for the visit.

Piping in the haggis at our Burns' night supper

Dressing up in clothes of long ago

This was followed up with small-world play and staff provided appropriate artefacts which encouraged this, with great success.

Playing 'Long long ago' with small-world artefacts

We have focused in this book on the importance of children learning about space and time and reasons for things. Here we see how with great skill staff have managed to offer children a sense of historic time, 'Long, long ago' in ways which carry meaning for young children still rooted in time present, but beginning to manage to reach out a bit into time past, providing it links with their own experiences of life.

Beyond the here and now

Children who have symbolic aspects to their lives live deeply, richly, flexibly, and are free from the here and now, able to transform into the past and future, experimenting and adapting. They learn what makes a personal symbol, and which are the shared conventions of their community and the wider world of time, space and reason. These children are equipped to travel competently and will have the skills for uncertain futures.

In practice

- How rich is the cultural life of your setting? It can only be as rich as the adults who work in it. How seriously do you work at your own professional and personal development?
- Do you study and participate in cultural events? Do you read literature, including poetry and non-fiction material, which helps you to think about the world and people beyond yourself in space and time?
- Do you participate in culture, from dancing to music, art to drama, travel, learning other languages, gaining insight into other ways of dressing, social rituals, religious beliefs, or ways of living a good life which do not involve any deities?
- How do you share this with the children and families you work with? If you dance, do you dance in the group setting? If you make music in your leisure time, do you share it at work in the setting?
- If you enjoy art, do you provide opportunities to share this with children?
- Do you impose your agenda on the children? Remember, each artist is an individual. No two dancers, musicians, choreographers, composers, creative scientists, mathematicians, dramatists, writers, poets, will do things the same way. We are each as unique as our finger-prints.
- Do you set up opportunities for children to develop their personal and unique symbols, or do you only give them activities in which they have to carry out your preconceived tasks? If so, they will just become cogs in a factory, and manufacture your ideas, losing their own as they do so.

Further reading

Asquith, T. (2001) 'The Development of Writing in the Nursery', *Early Childhood Practice: The Journal for Multi-Professional Partnerships* 3(1): 55–66.

Davies, M. (2003) *Movement and Dance in Early Education*, 2nd edn. London: Paul Chapman Publishing.

Duffy, B. (1998) *Supporting Creativity and Imagination in the Early Years*. Buckingham: Open University Press.

Gura, P., ed. (1992) *Exploring Learning: Young Children and Blockplay*. London: Paul Chapman Publishing.

Matthews, J. (2003) *Drawing and Painting: Visual Representation*, 2nd edn. London: Paul Chapman Publishing.

Pound, L. and Harrison, C. (2002) *Supporting Musical Development in the Early Years*. Maidenhead: Open University Press.

Whitehead, M. (1999) 'A Literacy Hour in the Nursery? The Big Question Mark', *Early Years* 19(2): 51–61.

Whitehead, M. (2002) *Developing Language and Literacy with Young Children*, 2nd edn. London: Paul Chapman Publishing.

Worthington, M. and Carruthers, E. (2002) *Children's Mathematics: Making Marks, Making Meaning*. London: Paul Chapman Publishing.

11

Learning in Childhood and Beyond: Charlie's day

> **Key themes**
>
> The importance of working in partnership with parents and carers is central in developing the learning of young children.
>
> This is a two-way process, and just as early-childhood practitioners will need to inform parents about their observations of children, and plans for working with them, so parents will need to feel comfortable in sharing their knowledge of their children with staff, carers and childminders.
>
> The diversity of people is far reaching in its implications for working with children. Yet, despite the differences between people culturally, in gender, ethnicity, disability, linguistically, every child needs to feel a sense of belonging, and to know they are a unique individual, who matters and is valued.
>
> In this chapter, we see how Charlie's learning, especially through mark making and choices of books, is valued, recognized and developed both in his independent learning and at group times.

In this chapter we meet Charlie, whose family is South Korean. He and his sister Judy have joined the Princess Elizabeth Nursery School.

Setting off from home

Charlie's mum helps Charlie, who will be five in the summer, and his sister Judy, to pack their books into the plastic folders and then into her shopping bag. Charlie has borrowed a book about frogs from the nursery, and Judy has a book of nursery rhymes.

Being greeted

Just as in Chapter 1 Christopher and his mum were warmly and individually greeted when they arrived at the family centre, so Charlie, his sister Judy and his mum are made to feel noticed and valued as they arrive. Staff take it in turns to welcome families and tick them off on the attendance register.

To be ignored affects self-esteem (Roberts, 2002). If this continues, we begin to feel that we do not matter. We tend to focus our attention on children and families who grab our attention, because they challenge us, or because they are socially skilled and at ease in talking in English with staff. Charlie's mum is quiet in manner, and so are her children. It would be easy to overlook their needs in a busy start to the nursery day.

The gender aspects of choosing books

Charlie (like some boys) is attracted to books which are non-fictional more than books which have stories and rhymes. He has enjoyed studying tadpoles and seeing them develop into frogs at school. He has drawn pictures of frogs, and he has written his name on the page opposite his drawing.

During the year Charlie has borrowed 22 books from the school. Nine of these were non-fiction books, including books about animals, eating fruit, Muslim faith, history, the stars and submarines. Two are books of rhymes, 11 are stories.

It is interesting to discover that of the books he chose to borrow nine were non-fiction. As he has become more experienced and has more idea about the kinds of books he finds interesting and rewarding to read, he is able to exert more choice and his preferences begin to show.

It is very important to provide children with choices of both fiction and non-fiction books to read and borrow. If mainly fiction books are provided with stories dominating more than poetry and rhyme, and there are few non-fiction books on offer, then boys are likely to lose out (Barrs and Pidgeon, 2002). Of course, not all boys prefer non-fiction, so it is important not to stereotype books into being suitable for boys or girls. What is important is to:

- introduce all children to fiction (stories, poetry and rhymes);
- introduce all children to non-fiction;
- respect and encourage their developing choices;
- create balance by finding poems and stories to resonate with non-fiction;
- create balance by finding non-fiction that complements stories and poems;
- make sure that children are helped to tease out the differences in fiction, with poetic licence, story genres and conventions, and the fact and accuracy of non-fiction.

The importance of not stereotyping by gender

It is often reported by practitioners that the boys they work with prefer to engage in three-dimensional rather than two-dimensional endeavours (Gura, 1992). They like to build models and constructions or engage in outdoor activity with vigorous movement. Certainly male brains (Carter, 1998) often seem to develop spatial concepts very readily. However, this is not necessarily the case. It is always best to carefully observe individual children, and to tune into their best ways of developing learning.

When children are treated as individuals, the gender aspects become less dominant. It is when boys feel anxious about doing 'girly' things that they take evasive action. When learning environments are set out to attract different sorts of people, then this pressure disappears, and children are able to be themselves. Boys begin to draw, paint and dance, and play with dolls, among other things.

Certainly, and rather obviously, there are biological differences between boys and girls learning and developing. Just as boys are more spatially directed, so girls talk more readily. Boys and girls move differently. However, the cultural aspects of the differences between boys and girls are another huge factor in developing learning.

The importance of not stereotyping by culture

Charlie arrived from South Korea when he was just four years old. He is returning there with his family now that he is about to be five.

Cultural stereotypes, like gender stereotypes, narrow our way of looking at children and their families. Living in a multiplicity of cultural contexts is not unusual for many children, especially in large post-industrial cosmopolitan urban conglomerations. Charlie is doing this. He has already experienced living in two different countries. He has broadened his circle of relationships by joining the school community. He knows that in different places there are different ways of doing things.

Finding something familiar and comforting in a new situation

It is interesting that he chooses something safe to settle himself into new situations. His family encourages him to draw, and he finds this is also cultivated at school. There is a good atmosphere around mark making through painting and drawing. He is free to draw as he knows and feels able.

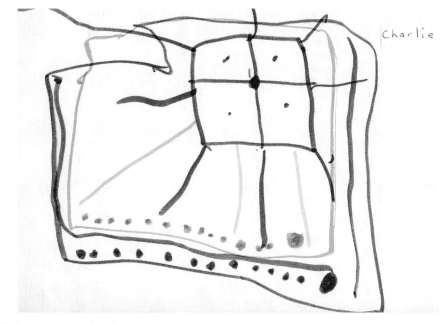

Enclosures, dabs and grids

We do not know if drawing will always be a great interest and love for him. It may be that he will branch out into other forms of symbol use as he begins to feel safe and to believe he can have a go at new things. This was certainly the case with his choices of books. We could really begin to see, across the year, his own individual interests developing. Cultural influences can constrain as much as they help children to participate in groups. It is those who branch out who are creative.

Children between the ages of four and six are very vulnerable in relation to the symbols they develop and use. This is because they are making connections across their own personal symbols and those which are the conventions of the cultures in which they dwell. If their experimentation closes down, they begin, for example, to settle on a few formulaic marks on paper. This may happen because adults direct them into tasks which have narrow possibilities, or when they are too anxious to have a go at using a wider range of materials more widely; they are receiving their culture, rather than participating in it and developing it. Children who are given templates, tracing activities and outlines to colour in are encouraged to become passive receivers. Only the exceptional can, under those circumstances, retain their creative possibilities.

Most cultures do not actively encourage creativity in drawing. Instead craftsmanship is cultivated, and children are taught well-known formulae.

This has been criticized by educators such as John Matthews (2003), and the creativity with enthusiasm for drawing and painting in the many children he has taught is evident.

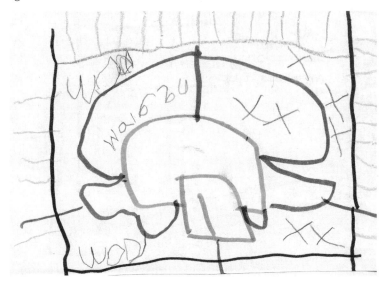

Arcs and spokes

Moments of transition

Charlie loves to draw. Because this is encouraged at home, when he arrives at school, he often begins his day at the drawing table. For him it is a way of making the transition from saying goodbye to his mum and settling into the nursery. His drawings show the well-being (Pascal and Bertram, 1999) he expresses in doing this, and the feeling of belonging (Carr, 2001) he has.

Charlie's experiments with mark making

His early drawings show grid formations and enclosures (Athey, 1990; Nutbrown, 1999), with carefully placed dabs. In his second term he begins to use more curved lines. They are not the simple circular enclosures he has been able to draw since he was about two years old. Nor are they the straight-sided enclosures he has been experimenting with lately. They are mixtures of the two. Across the next two months these more complex enclosures begin to be used as a central core, with arcs or spikes around it. Sometimes he separates these out into strips, which look like writing in sentences, although he does not call them sentences. He says it is writing. Sometimes he bends them round into curved strips.

Experiments with writing and numbers

Co-ordinating straight lines and curves to make the number 5.

His ability to place and turn lines and curves in combinations of directions into a co-ordinated drawing is developing rapidly. This shows in the people he draws, and is celebrated in being able to do a number 5. The joy of being able to switch from curve to line at will is huge for Charlie. It results in experiments with letters as well as drawings. Sometimes he writes his name all in capital letters. Sometimes he mixes capitals and lower case. Karmiloff-Smith (1992: 69) says, 'Children are not just problem-solvers. They are problem-generators.'

Fortunately, at the Princess Elizabeth Nursery School and at home, Charlie has been able to try out his experiments with two-dimensional drawing, painting, and writing letters and numbers. If he had been required to trace his name, use outlines drawn by adults for him to colour in, use templates or copy, he would not have been able to:

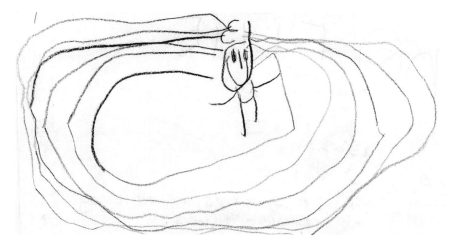

Now Charlie is using curves, he will enjoy finding lower-case letters

- experiment with the possibilities of making marks with paper, pencils and paint;
- find out how to make letters which connect with him and in particular those he has an emotional relationship with, such as his name;
- find out how to make numbers;
- feel ownership and control of the marks he makes, which gives him a sense of well-being, competency and technical skill, and means that he is finding his own voice and style;
- generate problems; he would have been stuck with solving problems set by other people in the form of adult-directed tasks.

Being allowed to make decisions and choices, and to take appropriate responsibility for doing so is an important aid to developing learning.

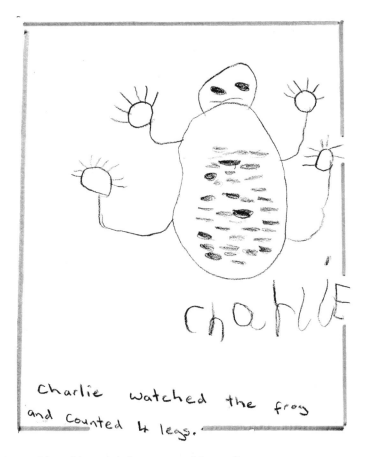

Charlie begins to pick out his name in lower-case and draw a frog

Changing from one kind of learning to another – transitions again

Having spent some time deeply involved in drawing, Charlie finds his coat and goes outside. As so often happens, when transitioning from one kind of learning to another, children need a bit of time to reorientate. Charlie spends about five minutes walking about outside, before stepping on and off the circle of logs with other children. His access strategies (Corsaro, 1979) for joining the play of others is well-established, and so he does not ask to join, nor does he look anxious. Having watched the play for a while from a distance, he knows what is involved, and simply imitates the others. The boy nearest to him turns and smiles as he joins in.

Balancing solo, companionship and interactive learning with others

After a few more minutes, he leaves and goes to the slide for more solo play. He knows how to climb the slide safely. He then goes indoors to the jigsaw table, which is set out in a time-honoured tradition. This involves double provision.

Double provision

Charlie, as many children do, settles into a change of learning by using a well-established strategy. He has been able to do the puzzles with insets for a long time, but he finds this helps him into doing jigsaws in a comfortable way. The nursery nurse, Joyce, does not challenge him by pointing out that this puzzle is too easy for him. The picture on the puzzle is linked to their work on tadpoles and their metamorphosis into frogs. When he has done this puzzle, he repeats it several times and then reaches for the second puzzle. This is a more complicated puzzle of a pond scene. He uses the strategy of finding the straight edges to make the picture from the outside in. He has more difficulty finding the inside matches. Joyce shows him the picture on the box, and he begins to use this to look for the heads of frogs or water-lily pads and flowers. Joyce's skill lies in knowing when to help and when not to help.

Charlie playing on the logs

Because the puzzles table is organized by hierarchical difficulty, children can access it at the right level for them. They can choose whether to relax with a puzzle or seek a challenge. Adults can support them accordingly, based on careful observation. Charlie also knows that he can take any puzzle from the shelf near the puzzle table, if he prefers. In this way, he is continually offered difficult and easier puzzles, and new and familiar puzzles.

From solo and companionship play to interactive play

Charlie leaves the puzzles and goes to the mat where his friend is playing with the small-world cars on the floor. He chooses not to use the roads set out on the floor map, and instead fetches some unit blocks and makes his own road out of them. Pre-structured equipment curtails choice and narrows the range of possibilities for use. The map does not invite the same level of thinking about how to make roads for cars as blocks. The thinking has been done for the children, and so they do not think. Charlie seems to know that, and so avoids the map, preferring to do his own thinking about where he wants to put roads. The two children talk about this, and the scene is one of constant change, reflecting their flexible, flowing thinking. The play is joined by a girl, who begins to place shops and houses along the road. This is welcomed by the boys.

Getting the balance of the day right for individual children and families

So far we have seen Charlie choosing to engage with a wide variety of the material provision and experiences which form part of the structured learning environment in which he spends time. It is evident that Charlie, like most children, develops his learning to an amazing degree through being encouraged to go where his interests lead him. When he needs more help and support, then it is often forthcoming from ever observant and highly trained adults, or from his parents who are tuned into his interests. His dad makes time to play football with him at home, knowing how much he enjoys developing the techniques of making contact with and kicking the ball, or targeting it.

Cross-cultural studies (Whiting and Edwards, 1992; Konner, 1991; Sharp, 2002) point to the likelihood that children in nomadic, settled agricultural or post-industrial societies benefit from spending about three-quarters of their time following their interests, developing learning through play, socializing and helping with everyday daily living tasks. There are enormous cultural variations in the forms these experiences will take, with huge diversity even within countries and families. In short, there are many ways of growing up.

Meeting the child's needs as identified by their society

Children are connected to the cultural context in which they grow up, whether or not this is a comfortable process. Children growing up in war-torn areas, poverty, homes where there is a constant state of quarrelling, or where they are made anxious with pressure to perform early and well, do not experience the kinds of atmosphere which favour the easy development of learning.

Charlie and his sister will experience a different system of education on their return to South Korea. If they had attended a nursery in a different part of the UK they would have been exposed to a different curriculum framework from the Scottish one. The experiences children have sculpt the way that their learning develops in ways which are deeply intertwined with the people they meet, the places they grow up, and the cultural atmosphere of their family and the wider community.

Tried and tested traditions

The list of experiences on p. 208 will put children in touch with seasonal rhythms and help them to interact with and understand the natural world.

Other important strands included in the staff's plans involve music, movement and dance, together with the acting out of stories with their narratives and characters. Children need to know what music is, how dances are made, and what is needed to make a story. They also, and in resonance and parallel, need to be encouraged to try out making their own dances, music and stories. Each feeds off the other. All of this rich, deep and broad experience supports and strengthens the development of literacy and numeracy. At times being aware of these processes helps the learning. At other times, children need to be supported in working at an intuitive level, where the awareness is not open to being articulated through words.

Daily-life learning is another powerful way of supporting and cultivating and developing the learning of young children, are naturally and biologically disposed to seek out and actively want to take part in the everyday life of their cultural context.

Charlie has daily opportunities to bake, make snacks, try out woodwork or to sew and take care of the materials. He also engages in experiences with traditional provision such as wooden blockplay.

Cultural variations in the curriculum

Although there are cultural variations in the UK and other post-industrial countries in the way that children are offered experiences which develop their learning, there are also similarities. Children growing up in the rest of Europe participate in similar experiences, as do children in early-years settings in New Zealand, where the *Te Whariki Curriculum Framework* is in place, or Australia, the US and the Nordic countries.

Charlie and the children in this book are learning in ways which have been tried and tested in many parts of the world. The way that the materials are offered and structured, and the way that children are valued as individuals who belong to a family and a community, demonstrates the cultural aspects of developing learning. A curriculum framework reflects the culture in which the child learns.

The *Te Whariki* framework is a bicultural one, which values both Maori and Pakeha (white) people. Practitioners are now working to make it diverse enough to include the cultures of the seven Pacific Island countries whose children are growing up in New Zealand.

The Welsh, Northern Irish and Scottish curriculum frameworks emphasize the history, music, dance, story and poetry of those countries. The *Curriculum Guidance for the Foundation Stage* (DFES/QCA, 2000) in England, has been hard-won, giving protection to children from early formal-skills teaching in diverse early years settings, but especially in reception classes. It is exerting an upward influence on yr 1 of the primary school.

Sharing the curriculum with parents and family

The Home-School book charting Charlie's progress through the Princess Elizabeth Nursery School links him to the Scottish priorities for meeting his needs. There is emphasis on working with his family, building on his learning through observation embedded in the staff's knowledge of child development and pedagogy, across the five areas of:

- Emotional, Personal and Social Development
- Communication and Language
- Knowledge and Understanding of the World

- Physical Development and Movement
- Expressive and Aesthetic Development.

In early years settings throughout the UK staff often plan work with the children, which they share with parents. At the beginning of the Home–School book, parents are advised that during the summer term, for example, there will be practical work with the children in the following:

- Spring to Summer: Be aware of change and its effect
- Sowing seeds for planting out in the garden
- Growing plants for the garden
- Planting potatoes and summer bulbs
- Work in the Nursery Garden
- Butterfly Life Cycle
- Frog Life Cycle
- Local Walks
- Visits to the shop for provisions for snack-time and baking
- Friday friends, health visitor, dental nurse and others
- Music at the piano using music cards (made by Charlie's Mum)
- Visits to community centre for small apparatus, music and movement
- Nursery rhymes – the Spanish way
- Children's Festival theatre trip
- Visits from Primary School staff to Nursery
- Visits to Primary School by Nursery staff
- Welcoming new families
- People who help us
- Garden games
- Holidays and travel
- Parental consultations
- Moving onto School
- Maps and photographs ready to celebrate Open Day
- Preparing to be garden guides
- Family outing to Pittencrieff Park, Dunfermline
- Leavers' Certificates and handing over the Home–School book to leavers.

Group times that are not too formal or adult-dominated

At the end of the morning, Charlie joins a group of a dozen children for story-time, songs and action rhymes. Action rhymes come from the early traditions developed by Froebel, although nowadays the original ones are not used, as they have been replaced with more relevant ones for modern children.

The teacher has chosen the story of 'Goodnight Owl' by Pat Hutchins. Charlie enjoys joining in with the catchphrase. He sits at the edge, outside the main zone of interaction, and so the teacher needs to be aware and to help him remain involved. She asks him to hold the owl puppet, and to put it in the tree as she reads the story.

He enjoys the action songs. The teacher asks the children what they would like to sing next. The response from the children is typical, choosing well-worn, easy and comfortable songs, 'Baa, Baa, Black Sheep', and 'Twinkle Twinkle, Little Star'. Ouvry (2002, personal communication) emphasizes the importance of giving children a balance of easier and more challenging songs to sing. With support, four-year-olds can often manage simple rounds, such as 'London's Burning', or the spring-time madrigal, 'Summer is a coming in'.

Knowing names

The teacher also plays some games which help the children to know each other by name as well as staff. It is important that children are not herded into large groups, but can retain their individuality by remaining themselves. When children do not have to leave themselves behind through being part of a group, they are more relaxed, and this helps them to become more aware of and sensitive to the needs of others. Knowing the names of people and finding out about them in discussion with the group supports this kind of learning. It is a very big emotional step to join a group. Charlie reacts by sitting quietly, but he needs encouragement to participate. Other children feel a loss of self, and try to exert control of the situation by engaging in a two-way conversation with the adult as if no one else is there. Others find interaction with the adult too pressured and so they begin a conversation with children around them, to take attention away from the adult as the focus. These are very understandable responses.

Ergonomics and group times

If group times with large numbers of eight or more children under the age of six are to be effective in developing learning, then they need to be physically active. We saw in earlier chapters that the developing brain feeds off information from the senses and movement.

Sitting comfortably

Sitting still is bad for children (Goddard-Blythe, 2000). Ergonomics are very important. Physiotherapists stress posture as part of active sitting (Curtis and Curtis, 2002) Young children need the correct size of chair to sit on, or bean bags and cushions which allow them to keep adjusting. They should never be required to sit, even actively, for longer than 10–20 minutes. Adults working with young children should take care to sit correctly, and chairs in the story area should be carefully designed to encourage this.

Oxygen, fresh air and water

Just as the way that Charlie sits and is not constrained to move while developing his learning, so his brain is also opened up to maximum learning because he has spent time in the open air in the garden. The brain feeds on oxygen as well as information from the senses and movement.

It is also important for his learning that there is a table in the nursery at child height with a jug of water and named cups for children to help themselves whenever they feel thirsty. The brain benefits from water at regular intervals.

Charlie goes home; the key person

At the end of the session Charlie's mum comes to collect him and his sister Judy. She has a little chat with the member of staff who is the key worker for Charlie and his family. This practitioner maintains the records on Charlie in his Home–School Book, and makes a special link with his parents. Key person systems (Elfer, 1996; Manning-Morton and Thorp, 2003; Forbes, in press) are usually found in settings working with children from birth to three, but they are fast becoming established in settings for children from three to five. In many settings the key person leads the home visits with the family, and goes with children for transitional visits when children move from the early years setting to primary school.

When he gets home, Charlie is pleasantly tired. He has a meal with his mother and sister, Judy, and then has a sleep. When his dad comes home, they go outside and play football together.

Including everyone

Charlie has a sense of belonging in his family. He is shown that he is valued, and that he matters, as a unique person, with individual needs. The bonding of boys with their father, or girls with their mother, is an important part of developing learning (Biddulph, 1997). Children of gay and lesbian parents are not necessarily gay or lesbian, just as in families with heterosexual parents children may be gay or lesbian. In the UK we are only just beginning to develop knowledge and understanding of these diversities in families. We have much to learn about gender and sex roles in the modern context. Charlie is growing up with South Korean roots, but is at ease in the culture of his community in the UK. It is important that the staff of the nursery school continually strive to implement in practice principles relating to equalities, diversity and inclusion.

Terminology is important, because it reflects attitudes and values. Children who are different for any reason at all are still part of the community, and they need to feel that this is so.

In practice

- How closely do you work in partnership with the parents and carers of each child?
- Are they involved in recording the child's progress?
- Do you encourage children to reflect on their own learning? Do you, the parents and carers and the child, gather together important photographs (of dancing, making music, models, free-flow play), drawings, paintings and mark-making, and show the journey of the child's learning in a large book?
- Do you invite the receiving teachers or practitioners to visit and share these with you and the family?
- Do you keep in mind that the best teaching emerges when you constantly develop your expertise in observation, and use it to inform what you do next and plan?
- Do you constantly work at providing support in learning with a rich material environment indoors and outdoors? This needs to be sustained or the environment will soon look shabby and disorganized.
- Do you use this as a base to extend the provision as a particular need arises?
- Do you work as a team? Who takes responsibility for what? How do you meet to discuss and plan together? Does everyone have to write everything down, or can you share the planning?

- Do you make sure that the children have things on the plan which will engage and involve them in their learning?
- Do you find that you enjoy your work more and that children learn more when you think of them as individual people with families rather than as a group of children who all need to be put through a string of activities?

Further reading

Athey, C. (1990) *Extending Thought in Young Children: A Parent-Teacher Partnership*. London: Paul Chapman Publishing.

Carr, M. (1999) 'Being a Learner: Five Learning Dispositions for Early Childhood', *Early Childhood Practice: The Journal for Multi-Professional Practice* 1(1): 81–100.

Dunkin, J. and Hanna, P. (2001) *Thinking Together: Quality Adult/Child Interactions*. Wellington, NZ: New Zealand Council for Educational Research.

Key themes

The title of this book, *Developing Learning in Early Childhood*, reflects its key themes. We have seen some of the values, issues, research and theory which help us to support and actively help children and their families to develop their learning about ideas, thoughts, feelings, relationships and embodiment, during childhood and beyond.

Childhood lasts forever. It has a past, present and future, which begin in early childhood. In this book we have explored how we can do our best to make sure that whatever the future holds for a child growing up, that child will be equipped (through the help they have had in developing their learning) to find positive, proactive, fulfilling ways forward.

Bibliography and references

Abbott, L. and Moylett, H. (1997a) *Working with the Under Threes: Responding to Children's Needs*. Maidenhead: Open University Press.

Abbott, L. and Moylett, H. (1997b) *Working with the Under Threes: Training and Professional Development*. Maidenhead: Open University Press.

Abbott, L. and Nutbrown, C. (2001) *Experiencing Reggio Emilia: Implications for Pre-School Provision*. Maidenhead: Open University Press.

Acredelo, L. and Goodwyn, S. (1997) *Baby Signs*. London: Hodder and Stoughton.

Ainsworth, M. and Wittig, B. (1969) 'Attachment and Exploratory Behaviour of One-Year-Olds in a Strange Situation', in B. Foss (ed.) *Determinants of Infant Behaviour*, Vol. 4, pp. 111–36. London: Methuen.

Arnold, C. (1999) *Child Development and Learning 2–5 Years: Georgia's Story*. London: Paul Chapman Publishing.

Asquith, T. (2001) 'The Development of Writing in the Nursery', *Early Childhood Practice: The Journal for Multi-Professional Partnerships* 3(1): 55–66.

Athey, C. (1990) *Extending Thought in Young Children: A Parent-Teacher Partnership*. London: Paul Chapman Publishing.

Bailey, D., Bruer, J., Symons, F. and Lichtman, J. (eds) (2001) *Critical Thinking about Critical Periods*. Baltimore, MD: Paul Brookes Publishing.

Bain, A. and Barnett, L. (1980) *The Design of a Day Care System in a Nursery Setting for Children Under Five*. London: Tavistock Institute for Human Relations.

Baker, M. (2001) 'Narrative Observation Notes'. Children's House Nursery School: Castlebrae Community Cluster. Unpublished.

Barrs, M. and Pidgeon, S., eds (2002) *Boys and Reading*. London: CLPE.

Bates, E. (1999) 'Tuning into Children'. BBC Radio 4, Programme 1. (*Time to Talk*).

Bateson, G. (1955) 'A theory of play and fantasy'. *Psychiatric Research Reports*, 2: 39–51.

Bekoff, M. and Byers, J. (eds) (1998) *Animal Play: Evolutionary, Comparative and Ecological Perspectives*, Cambridge: Cambridge University Press.

Bell, D. (ed.) (1999) Psychoanalysis and Culture: A Kleinian Perspective. London: Duckworth.

Bell, D. (2001/02) *Annual Report of Her Majesty's Chief Inspector of Schools, Standards and Quality in Education*. Norwich: OFSTED.

Bendall, K. (2003) 'This is Your life...', *New Scientist* (17 May): 1–4.

Biddulph, S.(1997) *Raising Boys*. London: Thorsons.

Bilton, H. (1998) *Outdoor Play in the Early Years: Management and Innovation*. London: David Fulton.

Bjørkvold, J.-R. (1992) *The Muse Within: Creativity and Communication, Song and Play from Childhood through Maturity*. New York: Harper Collins.

Blakemore, C. (2001) 'What Makes a Developmentally Appropriate Early Childhood Curriculum?'. Lecture given at the RSA (14 February).

Blakemore, S.J. (2000) *Early Years Learning*, Report no. 140 (June). London: Parliamentary Office of Science and Technology.

Bortfield, H. and Whitehurst, G. (2001) 'Sensitive Periods in First Language Acquisition', in D. Bailey, J. Bruer, F. Symons and J. Lichtman (eds) *Critical Thinking about Critical Periods*. Baltimore, MD: Paul Brookes Publishing.

Brehony, K.(2000) 'English Revisionist Froebelians and the Schooling of the Urban Poor', in M. Hilton and P. Hirsch (eds) *Practical Visionaries: Women, Education and Social Progress 1790–1930*. Harlow: Pearson Education.

Britton, J. (1987) 'Vygotsky's Contribution to Pedagogical Theory', *English in Education*, NATE (Autumn): 22–6.

Brookson, M. and Spratt, J. (2001) 'When We Have Choices, We Can Have Vision: An Exploration of Play Based on an Observation in Reggio Emilia', *Early Childhood Practice: The Journal for Multi-Professional Partnerships* 3(2): 11–24.

Brown, M. (1975) 'Children's House Nursery School', in A. Swanson, *The History of Edinburgh's Early Nursery Schools*. Edinburgh: British Association for Early Childhood Education.

Brown, S. (1998) 'Play as an Organising Principle: Clinical Evidence and Personal Observations', in M. Bekoff and J. Byers (eds) *Animal Play: Evolutionary, Comparative and Ecological Perspectives*. Cambridge: Cambridge University Press.

Bruce, T. (1991) *Time to Play in Early Childhood Education*. London: Hodder and Stoughton.

Bruce, T. (1996) *Helping Young Children to Play.* London: Hodder and Stoughton.

Bruce, T. (1997) *Early Childhood Education*, 2nd edn. London: Hodder and Stoughton.

Bruce, T. (2001a) *Learning Through Play: Babies, Toddlers and the Foundation Years*. London: Hodder and Stoughton.

Bruce, T. (2001b) 'Objects of Transition', *Early Childhood Practice: The Journal for Multi-Professional Partnerships* 3(1): 77.

Bruce, T., Findlay, A., Read, J. and Scarborough, M. (1995) *Recurring Themes in Education*. London: Paul Chapman Publishing.

Bruce, T. and Meggitt, C. (2002) *Childcare and Education*, 3rd edn. London: Hodder and Stoughton.

Bruer, J. and Symons, F. (2001) 'Critical Periods: Reflections and Future Directions', in D. Bailey, J. Bruer, F. Symons and J. Lichtman (eds) *Critical Thinking About Critical Periods*. Baltimore, MD: Paul Brookes Publishing.

Bruner, J. (1977) *The Process of Education*, 2nd edn. Cambridge, MA, and London: Harvard University Press.

Bruner, J. (1983) *Child's Talk: Learning to Use Language*. Oxford: Oxford University Press.

Bruner, J.S. (1996) *The Culture of Education*. Cambridge, MA: Harvard University Press.

Buhler, C. (1931) The Social Behaviour of the Child in H. Milford (ed.) *Handbook of Child Psychology*. Worcester, MA: Clark University Press and London, Oxford University Press.

Burlingham, D. and Freud, A. (1942) *Young Children in War-Time: A Year's Work in a Residential War Nursery*. London: George Allen and Unwin.

Burman, E. (1994) *Deconstructing Developmental Psychology*. London: Routledge.

Calvin, W. (1996) *How Brains Think: Evolving Intelligence: Then and Now*. London: Weidenfeld and Nicolson.

Carr, M. (1999) 'Being a Learner: Five Learning Dispositions for Early Childhood', *Early Childhood Practice: The Journal for Multi-Professional Partnerships*, 1(1): 81–100.

Carr, M. (2001) *Assessment in Early Childhood Settings: Learning Stories*. London: Paul Chapman Publishing.

Carter, R. (1998) *Mapping the Mind*. London: Seven Dials.

Carter, R. (2002) *Consciousness*. London: Weidenfeld and Nicolson.

Chomsky, N. (1975) *Reflections on Language*. New York: Pantheon Books.

Christiansen, A. (2002) 'Play, Imagination and Communication: Analyses of Mobile Phone Play', *Early Childhood Practice: The Journal for Multi-Profes-

sional Partnerships 4(2): 50–61.

Clarke, P. (1992) *English as a Second Language in Early Childhood*. Victoria, Australia: Free Kindergarten Association.

Clarke, A. and Clarke, A. (2000) *Early Experience and the Life Path*. London: Jessica Kingsley Open Books.

Coles, R. (1992) *Anna Freud: The Dream of Psychoanalysis*. Wokingham, UK, and Reading, MA: Addison-Wesley.

Collinson, D. (1988) *Fifty Major Philosophers: A Reference Guide*. London: Routledge.

Corsaro, W. (1979) '"We're Friends, Right?" Children's Use of Access Rituals in a Nursery School', *Language in Society* 8: 315–36.

Curtis, C. and Curtis, M.T. (2002) *Active Sitting*. London: Sprint Physiotherapy Publications.

Dahlberg, G., Moss, P. and Pence, A. (1999) *Beyond Quality in Early Childhood Education and Care*. London: Falmer Press.

Daniels, H. (2001) Vygotsky and Pedagogy. New York and London: Routledge Falmer.

David, T., Gooch, K., Powell, S. and Abbott, L. (2003) *Birth to Three Matters: A Framework to Support Children in Their Earliest Years*. London: DFES/Sure Start.

Davies, M. (2003) *Movement and Dance in Early Childhood*, 2nd edn. London: Paul Chapman Publishing.

DFES/QCA (2000) *Curriculum Guidance for the Foundation Stage*, (2002) *Birth to Three Matters: A Framework to Support Practitioners Working with Children in Their Earliest Years*. London: DFES/Sure Start Publications.

Dissanayake, E. (2000) *Art and Intimacy: How the Arts Began*. Seattle, WA and London: University of Washington Press.

Doherty-Sneddon, G. (2003) *Children's Unspoken Language*. London: Jessica Kingsley Publishers.

Donald, M. (2001) *A Mind So Rare: The Evolution of Human Consciousness*. New York: W.W. Norton.

Donaldson, M. (1978) *Children's Minds*. London: Fontana/Collins.

Drummond, M.J. (2000) 'Susan Isaacs' Pioneering Work in Understanding Children's Lives', in M. Hilton and P. Hirsch (eds) *Practical Visionaries: Women, Education and Social Progress 1790–1930*. Harlow: Pearson Education.

Duffy, B. (1998) *Supporting Creativity and Imagination in the Early Years*. Maidenhead: Open University Press.

Dunkin, J. and Hanna, (2001) *Thinking Together: Quality Adult/Child Interactions*. Wellington, NZ: New Zealand Council for Educational Research.

Dunn, J. (1988) *The Beginnings of Social Understanding*. Oxford: Blackwell.

Dunn, J. (1993) *Young Children's Close Relationships*. London and New Delhi: Sage.

Dunn, J. (1995) 'Studying Relationships and Social Understanding', in P. Barnes *Personal, Social and Emotional Development of Children*. Oxford: Blackwell/Open University Press, Maidenhead.

Edgington, M. (2002) *The Great Outdoors: Developing Children's Learning through Outdoor Learning Experiences*. London: Early Education.

Egan, K. (1997) *The Educated Mind: How Cognitive Tools Shape Our Understanding*. Chicago, IL, and London: University of Chicago Press.

Elfer, P. (1996) 'Building Intimacy Relationships with Young Children in Nurseries', *Early Years* 16(2): 30–4.

Elfer, P., Goldschmied, E. and Selleck, D. (2002) *Key Persons in Nurseries: Building Relationships for Quality Provision*. London: NEYN.

Elman, J., Bates, E., Johnson, M., Karmiloff-Smith, A., Parisi, D. and Plunkett, K. (1996) *Rethinking Innateness: A Connectionist Perspective on Development*, a Bradford Book. Cambridge, MA, and London: MIT Press.

EPPE – see Siraj-Blatchford and Sylva.

Erickson, F. (1996) 'Going for the zone: Social and cognitive ecology of teacher–student interaction in classroom conversations', in D. Hicks (ed.) *Discourse, Learning and Schooling*, pp. 29–62. New York: Cambridge University Press.

Erikson, E. (1963) *Childhood and Society*. London: Penguin.

Field, T. (1999) 'Tuning into Children'. BBC, Radio 4, Programmes 1–6. (*Time to Talk*).

Fisher, J. (2002) *Starting with the Child: Teaching and Learning from Three to Eight*, 2nd edn. Maidenhead: Open University Press.

Foley, K. (2000) 'Southway Community Recipe Books'. Southway Nursery School. Unpublished. Available from Southway Nursery School, Ampthill Rd, Bedford.

Forbes, R. (forthcoming) *Beginning to Play: Birth to Three*. Maidenhead: Open University Press.

Fraser-Gunn, L. and colleagues (2001) 'Narrative Observations'. Princess Alice Nursery School, Castlebrae Community Cluster. Unpublished.

Frith, U. (1992) *Autism: Explaining the Enigma*. Oxford: Blackwell.

Froebel, F. (1887) *The Education of Man*. New York: Appleton.

Gardner, H. (1993) *Frames of Mind*. London: HarperCollins.

Garvey, C. (1977) *Play*. London: Fontana/Open Books.

Gibbs, W.W. (2002) 'From Mouth to Mind: New Insights into How Language Warps the Brain', *Scientific American* (September): 14–16

Goddard-Blythe, S. (2000) 'First Steps to the Most Important ABC', *Times Educational Supplement* (7 January): 23.

Goldschmied, E. and Jackson, S. (1994) *People under Three: Young Children in Day Care* London: Routledge.

Gomes-Pedro, J., Nugent, K., Young, G. and Brazelton, T.B. (eds) (2002) *The Infant and Family in the Twenty-First Century*. New York/Hove, UK: Brunner-Routledge.

Gopnik, A., Meltzoff, A. and Kuhl, P. (1999) *How Babies Think*. London: Weidenfeld and Nicolson.

Goswami, U. (1998) *Cognition in Children*. Hove, Sussex: Psychology Press.

Greenfield, S. (2000) *Brain Story: Unlocking our Inner World of Emotions, Memories, Ideas and Desires*. London: BBC Worldwide.

Greenman, J. and Stonehouse, A. (1997) *Prime Times: A Handbook for Excellence in Infant and Toddler Programs*. Melbourne: Longman.

Griffin, S. (2003) '"Selecting a Pram" Which Encourages Communication Between Adults, Babies and Toddlers', *Early Childhood Practice: The Journal for Multi-Professional Partnerships* 5(1): 4–7.

Gura, P., (ed.), with Froebel Blockplay Research Group (1992) *Exploring Learning: Young Children and Blockplay*. London: Paul Chapman Publishing.

Gura, P. (1996) *Resources for Early Learning: Children, Adults and Stuff*. London: Paul Chapman Publishing.

Gussin Paley, V. (1984) *Boys and Girls: Superheroes in the Doll Corner*. Chicago, IL: University of Chicago Press.

Gussin Paley, V. (1986) *Mollie is Three*. Chicago, IL: University of Chicago Press.

Gussin Paley, V. (1990) *The Boy Who Would Be A Helicopter*. Cambridge, MA: University of Harvard Press.

Gussin Paley, V. (2001) *In Mrs. Tulley's Room: A Child Portrait*. Cambridge, MA: Harvard University Press.

Harding, S. (2001) 'What's Happening with the Bikes?', *Early Childhood Practice: The Journal for Multi-Professional Partnerships* 3(2): 24–42.

Harris, P. (2000) *The Work of the Imagination*. Oxford: Blackwell Publishers.

Hatherly, A. and Duncan, J.(1999) 'The Outdoor Play Project at Auckland College of Education'. New Zealand, Video.

Hebb, D. (1961) *The Organisation of Behaviour*. New York: John Wiley.

Hilton, M. and Hirsch, P. (2000) *Practical Visionaries: Women, Education and Social Progress 1790–1930*. Harlow: Pearson Education.

Hobson, P. (2002) *The Cradle of Thought: Exploring the Origins of Thinking*. London: Macmillan.

Holland, P. (2003) *We Don't Play with Guns Here: War, Weapon and Superhero Play in the Early Years*. London and Maidenhead: Open University Press.

Holmes, J. (1993) *John Bowlby and Attachment Theory*. London: Routledge.

Holt, L. (2002) In W. Gibbs 'From Mouth to Mind: New Insights into How Language Warps the Brain'. *Scientific American*, September: 14–16.

Hopkins, J. (1988) 'Facilitating the Development of Intimacy Between Nurses and Infants in Day Nurseries', *Early Child Development and Care* 33: 99–111.

Huizunga, J. (1949) *Homo Ludens: A Study of the Play Element in Culture*. London: Routledge and Kegan Paul.

Hutchins, P. (1993) *Goodnight Owl*. London: Jonathan Cape, Random House Group Ltd.

Hutt, C., Tyler, S., Hutt, J. and Christopherson, H. (eds) (1988) *Play, Exploration and Learning: A Natural History of the Pre-School*. London: Routledge.

Hyder, T. (forthcoming) *War, Conflict and Play*. Maidenhead: Open University Press.

Isaacs, N. (1930) 'Children's "Why?" Questions', in S. Isaacs *Intellectual Development in Young Children*, Appendix A. London: Routledge and Kegan Paul.

Isaacs, S. (1930) *Intellectual Growth in Young Children*. London: Routledge and Kegan Paul.

Isaacs, S. (1933) *Social Development in Young Children*. London: Routledge and Kegan Paul.

Iverson, P. (2002) In W. Gibbs 'From Mouth to Mind: New Insights into How Language Warps the Brain', *Scientific American*, September: 14–16.

Jamieson, J. (1975) 'Princess Elizabeth Child Garden', in A. Swanson, *The History of Edinburgh's Early Nursery Schools*. Edinburgh: British Association for Early Childhood Education.

Jenkinson, S. (2001) *The Genius of Play: Celebrating the Spirit of Childhood*. Stroud: Hawthorn Press.

Jennings, J. (2002) 'A Broad Vision and a Narrow Focus', *Early Childhood Practice: The Journal for Multi-Professional Partnerships* 4(1): 50–60.

Kalliala, M. (2004) *Children's Play Culture in a Changing World*. Maidenhead: Open University Press.

Karmiloff-Smith, A. (1992) *Beyond Modularity: A Developmental Perspective on Cognitive Science*, a Bradford Book. Cambridge, MA, and London: MIT Press.

Katz, L. and Chard, S. (1989) *Engaging Children's Minds: A Project Approach.* Norwood, NJ: Ablex Publishing.

Kegl, J. (1997) 'Silent Children ... New Language'. BBC Horizon (3 April).

Keynes, R. (2002) *Annie's Box: Charles Darwin, His Daughter and Human Evolution*. London: Fourth Estate.

Kitzinger, C. (1997) 'Born to be Good? What Motivates Us to be Good, Bad or Indifferent Towards Others?', *New Internationalist* (April): 15–17.

Kohan, G., ed. (1986) *The British School of Psychoanalysis: The Independent Tradition*. New Haven, CT, and London: Yale University Press.

Konner, M. (1991) *Childhood*. Boston, Toronto and London: Little, Brown.

Laevers, F., ed. (1994) *The Innovative Project 'Experiential Education' and the Definition of Quality in Education*. Leuven: Katholieke Universiteit.

Lamb, M. (2001) 'Narrative Observations from St Francis Primary School'. Castlebrae Community Cluster. Unpublished.

Lichtman, J. (2001) 'Developmental Neurobiology overview: Synapses, Circuits and Plasticity', in D. Bailey, J, Bruner, F, Symons and J. Lichtman (eds) *Critical Thinking above Critical Periods*. Baltimore, MD: Paul Brookes Publishing.

Liebschner, J. (1991) *Foundations of Progressive Education*. Cambridge: Lutterworth Press.

Liebschner, J. (1992) *A Child's Work: Freedom and Guidance in Froebel's Educational Theory and Practice*. Cambridge: Lutterworth Press.

Lofdahl, A. (2002) 'Children's Narratives in Play: "I Put This Rice Pudding Here, Poisoned, so that Santa Claus Will Come and Eat It!"', *Early Childhood Practice: The Journal for Multi-Professional Partnerships* 4(2): 37–47.

Long, A. (2001) 'Forget about the "Music" – Concentrate on the Children', *Early Childhood Practice: The Journal for Multi-Professional Partnerships* 3(1): 71–6.

Lyotard, J.F. (1979) *The Postmodern Condition: A Report on Knowledge*, trans. G. Bennington and B. Massumi. Minneapolis, MN: University of Minnesota Press.

McCormick, C. (2001) 'Narrative observations from Cameron House Nursery School'. Castlebrae Community Cluster. Unpublished

McKechnie, C. and Jessop, B. (2002) 'The Food for Tot Resource Pack'. Craigmillar Community Cluster. Unpublished.

McMillan, M. (1930) *The Nursery School* . London: Dent.

Magee, B. (1987) *The Great Philosophers*. London: BBC Books.

Maier, H. (1978) *Three Theories of Child Development*. New York: Harper and Row.

Makin, L. and Spedding, S. (2002) 'Supporting Parents of Infants and Toddlers as First Literacy Educators: An Australian Initiative', *Early Childhood Practice: The Journal for Multi-Professional Partnerships* 4(1): 17–27.

Mandler, J. (1999) 'Pre-verbal Representations and Language', in P. Bloom, M. Peterson, L. Nadel, M. Garrett, *Language and Space*. Cambridge, MA: MIT Press.

Manning-Morton, J. and Thorp, M. (2003) *Keytimes for Play: the First Three Years*. Maidenhead: Open University Press.

Manolson, A. (1992) *It Takes Two to Talk: A Parent's Guide to Helping Children to Communicate*. Toronto, Ontario: Hanen Centre.

Maslow, A. (1962) *Towards a Psychology of Being*. Princeton, NJ: Van Nostrand.

Matthews, J. (2003) *Drawing and Painting: Children and Visual Representation*, 2nd edn. London: Paul Chapman Publishing.

Meade, A. (2000) 'The Brain and Early Childhood Development', *Pitopito Korero* 23 (June): 7–11.

Meade, A. (2002) 'The Dilemmas of Pluralism', *New Zealand Journal of Infant and Toddler Education* 4(1): 2.

Meade, A. (2003) 'What Are the Implications of Brain Studies on Early Childhood Education?', *Early Childhood Practice: The Journal for Multi-Professional Partnerships* 5(2): 4–18.

Mithen, S. (2003) 'Mobile Minds', *New Scientist* (17 May): 40–2.

Moyles, J. (1989) *Just Playing? The Role and Status of Play in Early Childhood Education*. Maidenhead: Open University Press.

Murray, L. and Andrews, L. (2000) *The Social Baby: Understanding Babies' Communication from Birth*. Richmond, Surrey: CP Publishing.

Newson, E. and Newson, J. (1979) *Toys and Playthings: A Fascinating Guide to the Nursery Cupboard*. London: Penguin.

Nielsen, L. (1992) *Space and Self: Active Learning by Means of the Little Room*. Copenhagen, Denmark: Sikon (available RNIB, London).

Nutbrown, C. (1999) *Threads of Thinking: Young Children Learning and the Role of Early Education*, 2nd edn. London: Paul Chapman Publishing.

Orr, R. (2003) *My Right to Play: A Child with Complex Needs*. Maidenhead: Open University Press.

Ouvry, M. (2000) *Exercising Muscles and Minds*. London: Early Years Network.

Panter-Brick, C. (1998) *Biosocial Perspectives on Children*. Cambridge: Cambridge University Press.

Pascal, C. and Bertram, T. (1999) *Effective Early Learning: Case Studies in Improvement*. London: Paul Chapman Publishing.

Penman, A. (1975) 'Cameron House Nursery School, 1934', in A. Swanson *The History of Edinburgh's Nursery Schools*. Edinburgh: British Association for Early Education.

Peters, C. (2002) 'Communication', *Early Childhood Practice: The Journal for Multi-Professional Partnerships* 4(1): 44–50.

Piaget, J. (1947) *The Psychology of Intelligence*, trans. M. Piercy and D. Berlyne. London: Routledge and Kegan Paul.

Piaget, J. (1952) *Play, Dreams and Imitation*, trans. C. Gattegno and F. Hodgson. London: Routledge and Kegan Paul.

Piaget, J. (1964) *Six Psychological Studies*. London: University of London Press.

Pinker, S. (1995) *The Language Instinct: The New Science of Language and Mind*. London: Penguin.

Pound, L. (1998) *Supporting Mathematical Development in the Early Years*. Maidenhead: Open University Press.

Pound, L. and Harrison, C. (2002) *Supporting Musical Development in the Early Years*. Maidenhead: Open University Press.

Ratey, J. (2001) *A User's Guide to the Brain*. London: Little, Brown.

Rayner, R. and Riding, S. (1999) *Cognitive Styles and Learning Strategies*. London: David Fulton.

Rice, S. (1998) 'Luke's Story', in J. Dwfor-Davies, P. Camera and J. Lee (eds) *Managing Special Needs in Mainstream Schools: The Role of the SENCO*. London: David Fulton.

Rice, S. (2001) 'Luke's Story', *Early Childhood Practice: The Journal for Multi-Professional Partnerships* 3(2): 60–8.

Roberts, R. (2002) *Self-Esteem and Early Learning*, 2nd edn. London: Paul Chapman Publishing.

Rogoff, B. (1998) 'Cognition as a collaborative process', in D. Kuhn and R.S. Siegler (eds) *Handbook of Child Psychology, Volume 2: Cognition, Perception and Language*, pp. 679–744 New York: Wiley.

Rogoff, B., Paradise, R., Arauz, R.M., Correa-Chávez, M. and Angelillo, C. (2003) 'Firsthand learning through intent participation', *Annual Reviews of Psychology*, 54: 175–203.

Rutter, M. (1989) *Pathways from Childhood to Adult Life*. Journal of Child Psychology and Psychiatry, 30: 23–51.

Rutter, M. and Rutter, M. (1992) *Developing Minds*. London: Penguin.

Sharp, E. (2001) 'Narrative Observations'. Peffermill (Castleview) Primary School, Castlebrae Community Cluster. Unpublished.

Singer, D. and Singer, J. (1990) *The House of Make-Believe: Play and the Developing Imagination*. Cambridge, MA. Harvard University Press.

Siraj-Blatchford, I., Sylva, K., Melhuish, E., Sammons, P. and Taggart, B. (2002) Technical Papers 1–10, London: University of London, Institute of Education, DFEE.

Siraj-Blatchford, I., Sylva, K., Muttock, S., Gilden, R. and Bell, D. (2002) *Researching Effective Pedagogy in the Early Years*, DFES Research Report No. 356. Norwich: HMSO.

Spencer, H. (1861) *Education: Intellectual, Moral and Physical*. London: G. Manwaring.

Steels, L.(2002) 'First Words: Interview with Helen Phillips', *New Scientist Archive* (30 March).

Storr, A. *Solitude*. London: Penguin.

Swanson, A. (1975) *The History of Edinburgh's Early Nursery Schools*. Edinburgh: British Association for Early Childhood Education.

Tarlton, L. (2001) 'Narrative observations from Castlebrae Family Centre'. Castlebrae Community Cluster. Unpublished.

Teicher, M. (2002) 'Scars That Won't Heal: The Neurobiology of Child Abuse', *Scientific American* (March): 54–61.

Te Whariki (1996) Early Childhood Curriculum. New Zealand Ministry of Education. Wellington: Learning Media.

Trevarthen, C. (1997) 'The curriculum conundrum: Prescription versus the Comenius Principle', in A.W.A. Dunlop and A. Hughes (eds) *Pre-School Curriculum. Policy, Practice and Proposals*, pp. 62–81. Glasgow: University of Strathclyde.

Trevarthen, C. (1998) 'The Child's Need to Learn a Culture', in M. Woodhead, D. Faulkner and K. Littleton *Cultural Worlds of Early Childhood*. London and New York: Routledge in association with Open University Press.

Trevarthen, C. (2002a) 'Learning in companionship', *Education in the North: The Journal of Scottish Education*, New Series, Number 10, 2002 (Session 2002–2001), pp. 16–25. The University of Aberdeen, Faculty of Education.

Trevarthen, C. (2002b) 'Origins of musical identity: evidence from infancy for musical social awareness', in R. MacDonald, D.J. Hargreaves and D. Miell (eds) *Musical Identities*, pp. 21–38. Oxford: Oxford University Press.

Trevarthen, C. (2003) 'Infancy, mind in', in R. Gregory (ed.) *Oxford Companion to the Mind*. Oxford: Oxford University Press. (Revised Edition in press, 2003).

Trevarthen, C. and Logotheti, K. (1987) 'First symbols and the nature of human knowledge', in J. Montagnero, A. Tryphon and S. Dionnet (eds) *Symbolisme et Connaissance/Symbolism and Knowledge*. (Cahiers de la Fondation Archives Jean Piaget, No. 8). Fondation Archives Jean Piaget: Geneva, 65–92.

Trevarthen, C. and Malloch, S. (2002) 'Musicality and music before three: Human vitality and invention shared with pride'. *Zero to Three*, September 2002, 23(1): 10–18.

Tryphon, A. and Voneche, J., eds (1996) *Piaget-Vygotsky: The Social Genesis of Thought*. Hove, Sussex: Psychology Press.

Tychsen, L. (2001) 'Critical Periods for Development of Visual Acuity, Depth Perception and Eye Tracking', in D. Bailey, J. Bruer, F. Symons and J. Lichtman (eds) *Critical Thinking About Critical Thinking*. Baltimore, MD: Paul Brookes Publishing.

Vygotsky, L. (1978) *Mind in Society*. London and Cambridge, MA.: Harvard University Press.

Wall, K. (2003) *Special Needs and Early Years: A Practitioner's Guide*. London: Paul Chapman Publishing.

Warnock, G. (1987) 'Kant', in B. Magee, *The Great Philosophers*. London: BBC Books.

Wells, G. (1987) *The Meaning Makers*. London: Hodder and Stoughton.

Whalley, M. and the Pen Green Team (2001) *Involving Parents in Their Children's Learning*. London: Paul Chapman Publishing.

Whitehead, M. (1990) 'First Words. The Language Diary of a Bilingual Child's Early Speech', *Early Years* 10(2): 3–14.

Whitehead, M. (1999a) 'A Literacy Hour in the Nursery? The Big Question Mark', *Early Years* 19(2) (Spring): 51–61.

Whitehead, M. (2002) *Developing Language and Literacy with Young Children*, 2nd edn. London: Paul Chapman Publishing.

Whiting, B. and Edwards, C. (1992) *Children in Different Worlds: The Formation of Social Behaviour*. Cambridge, MA: Harvard University Press.

Winnicott, D. (1971) *Playing and Reality*. London: Penguin.

Wolf, D. and Gardner, H. (1978) 'Style and Sequence in Early Symbolic Play', in N. Smith and M. Franklin (eds) *Symbolic Functioning in Early Childhood*. Hillsdale, NJ: Lawrence Erlbaum Associates.

Wood, E. and Attfield, J. (1990) *Play, Learning and the Early Childhood Curriculum*. London: Paul Chapman Publishing.

Woodhead, M., Faulkner, D. and Littleton, K. (1998) *Cultural Worlds of Early Childhood*. London: Routledge/Open University Press.

Worthington, M. and Carruthers, E. (2003) *Children's Mathematics*. London: Paul Chapman Publishing.

Index